Street Furniture

Edition 2007

Author: Jacobo Krauel
Editorial Coordinator: Marianna Morales
Architecture advisor: Marta Rojals
Graphic design: Dimitris Kottas
Text: contributed by the companies,
translated and edited by William George,
Nuria Rodriguez and Judy Thomson

Jonqueres, 10, 1-5
08003 Barcelona, Spain
Tel.: +34 93 301 21 99
Fax: +34-93-301 00 21
E-mail: info@linksbooks.net
www.linksbooks.net

Street Furniture

LINKS

Index

Introduction

Ever since the beginning of modern civilization, the urbanization of public space has been a prevailing subject and a subject in a constant state of mutation. Besides the structures, buildings and dwellings that serve the full range of possible requirements, cities as well as villages need streets, parks and plazas in which the inhabitants can move, rest, play, or get together. In fact, many urban design theorists consider that the life-quality of a city's inhabitants depends on the proportion of shared space available and how it is used.

There is no doubt that the urban furniture plays a leading role in making people's presence in these areas more frequent, agreeable and comfortable. A well distributed arrangement of benches, street lamps or shade will contribute to making a plaza more accessible, encouraging a more positive and lively relation between its visitors. Thus, an obvious improvement will ensue, strengthening the social links throughout the neighborhood.

Although many of us only hurry through these spaces briefly on our way to somewhere else, hardly noticing the urban furniture, these accessories are in fact a crucial component, capable of making life much more comfortable. On the other hand, for those who make public space a prolongation of their home, whether they be children, teenagers, retired people or members of any other population group, the lack of these items to which we are all accustomed would be highly traumatic. Hence, in many cities, groups of people have created associations to protest about the neglect of their neighborhoods. There are many housing estates in which local authorities have ignored these requests and the situation of neglect has become extremely chronic compared to other more fortunate districts of the same city.

Indeed, urban furniture seems to have become vital for contemporary cities. Not only can these items become a distinctive feature of a neighborhood and of a town, like London's telephone boxes, but it is their design and the degree to which they address the solution to everyday problems that proves their validity. The adaptation to different spaces, the durability or resistance to harsh atmospheric conditions or vandalism, an item's versatility or multiple use and of course its aesthetic value that are a source of inspiration to architects and designers, who have carried out their projects within the public space of the streets, squares and parks of our urban environments.

In this book we have compiled a selection of the most recent and significant contributions to this field of design. Effective and contemporary urban furniture, with designs ranging from the most classical to the most experimental and futuristic, in form as in the implementation of new materials and finishes. Each item is completely illustrated with photographs and plans, together with a full explanation of the constructive details, dimensions and weight, the installation process and the maintenance required. It is all perfectly ordered according to the functions fulfilled, and the clear and attractive layout with a file-like presentation make it ideally easy and practical to consult. We believe this book to be a good alternative to the usual collection of catalogues, providing an interesting source of inspiration for Town Halls, municipalities, town planners, architects, builders and students alike, all of whom will have access to the contact data of the makers of the outstanding items offered in this volume.

Seats

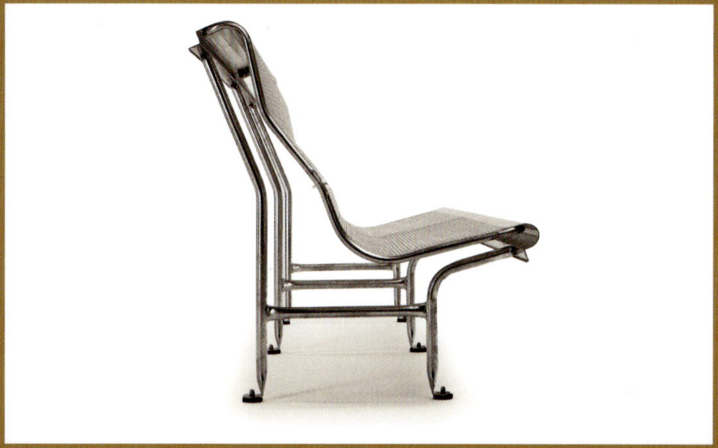
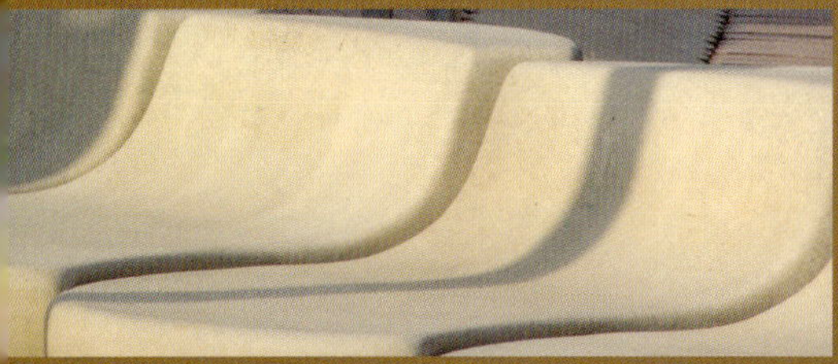

Cuc

Design: Foreign Office Architects (FOA) - Farshid Moussavi & Alejandro Zaera Polo
Production: mago: urban

Mago: urban produces and commercializes the Cuc bench. It was designed by Alejandro Zaera, Spain's most international architect, who made a name for himself among the world's top architects with his project for the passenger port terminal at Yokohama (Japan).

This bench was designed to be inserted within the paving system of the Auditoria of Barcelona Park, one of the emblematic spaces of the Forum of Cultures. The paving system of the Auditoria of Barcelona Park consists of a collection of pieces that, placed one after the other and rotating on their own axes, can adapt to any sort of terrain, however irregular. The bench in this park could not conform to straight lines or Cartesian geometry, as the paving was designed to adapt to the sinuous edges of the dunes that are in the park. And this was the basic idea behind the Cuc bench.

The seating unit, made of concrete, consists of a round surface of trunco-conical or tapered geometry that has a groove on one of its sides, which supports and locks the next unit, and so on. The surface of the seat rises to become a small, radially sloped backrest..

The Cuc bench has the characteristic of enabling multiple compositions simply by rotating each of the units that it is composed of. The main advantage being that it is possible to construct straight and curved structures by adding elements. Thus, we can say that it is a bench that makes a project more flexible as more elements can be added or its geometrical configuration restudied even after being fitted.

The bench is made in three colours: white, granite grey and ochre.

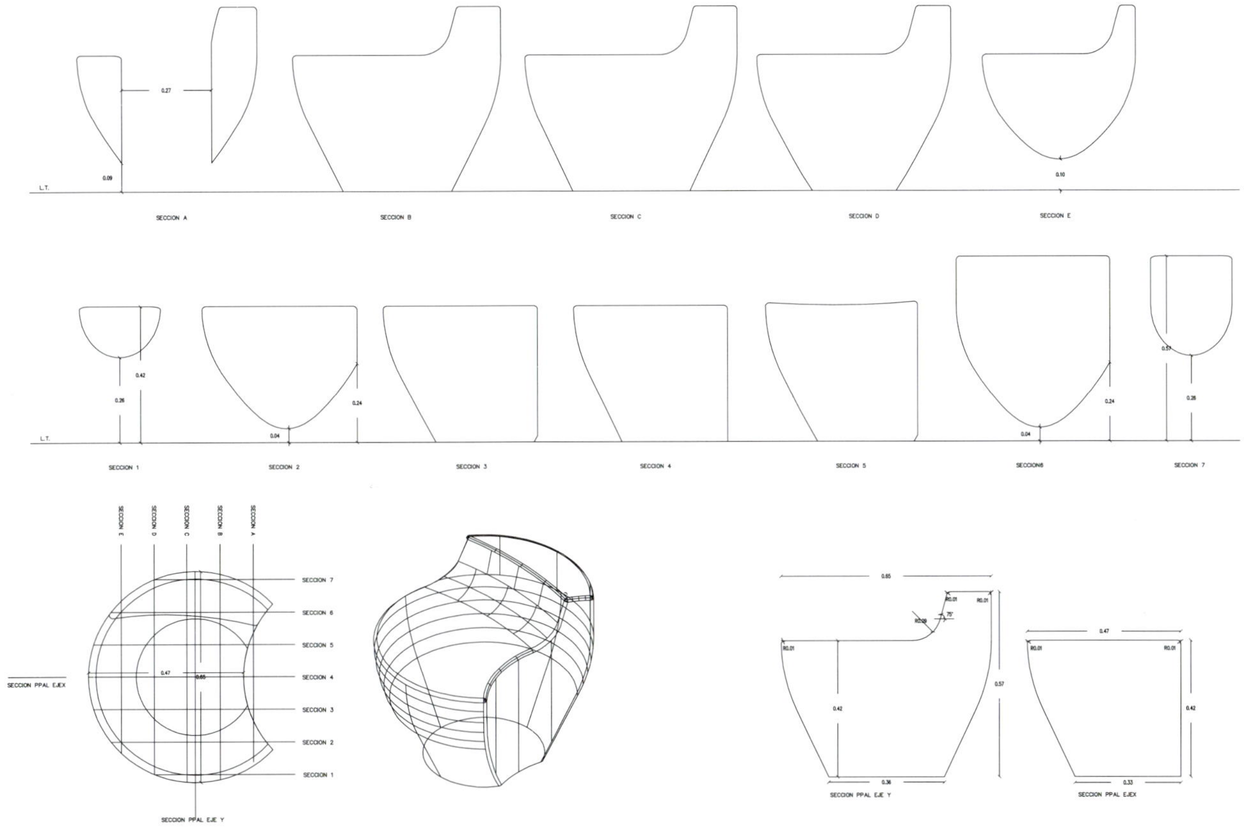
L.T.
SECCION A
SECCION B
SECCION C
SECCION D
SECCION E
SECCION 1
SECCION 2
SECCION 3
SECCION 4
SECCION 5
SECCION6
SECCION 7
SECCION PPAL EJE X
SECCION PPAL EJE Y

Hoja

Design: Diana Cabeza Collaborators: L. Heine I A. Ferrugia
Production: Estudio Cabeza

This urban bench is specially designed for resting or reading in an open public space or a partially-roofed area, like a plaza, a patio or a gallery.

As a result of the distinct architectural independence between the seat and the backrest and the various lengths in which both units are available, the Hoja bench offers multiple options – as a large back support for someone sitting on the floor, as rest support for a standing person or as a space where a pram or a wheel chair can be placed. The back of this bench constitutes a large vertebrate surface, acting as an ergonomic support.

Standard size

210 x 76.2 x h=40.5cm

backrest height = 89.5cm

Materials

Seat and backrest: in solid hardwood with penetrating sealer, natural finish.

Leg supports: Cast iron.

Finishing: Polyester thermosetting powder coating.

Fixing

Provided with steel sheet to embed into a buried concrete block.

Alternative: fixed with mechanical or chemical anchor bolts directly to the floor.

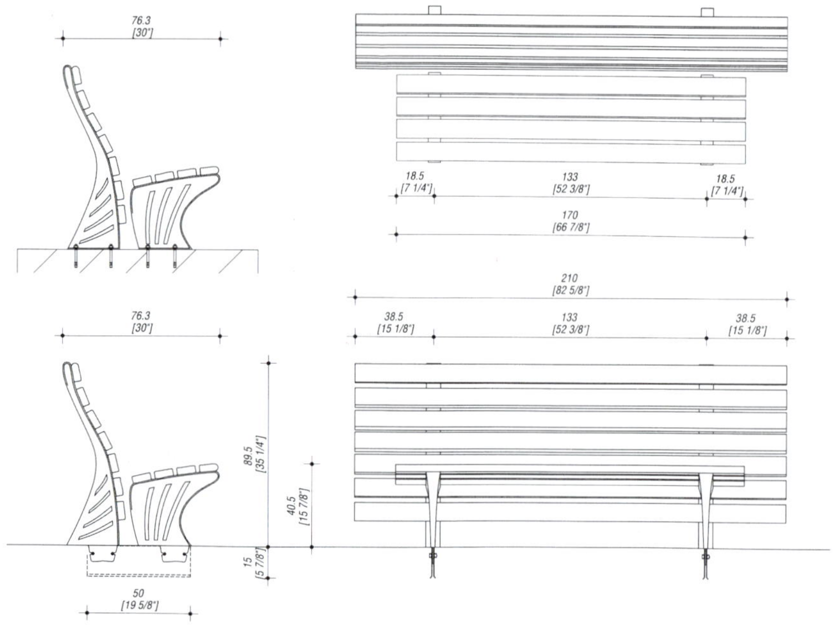

Trasluz

Design: Francisco J. Mangado
Production: DAE

The seat of this bench consists of eleven Iroko wood slats and a base formed by a box and lid in 10mm welded galvanized steel. The wooden slats which are 1,996 mm long and 40 mm wide by 25 mm are treated with a first coat of varnish primer and two coats of clear stained varnish with a satin-finish, based on acrylic resins in an aqueous phase emulsion. The box is finished with a coat of bi-component phosphate primer and a polyester resin based powder coating for outdoor performance. The standard colors are black and iron-effect steel grey. It weighs approximately 200 kg. The lighting comes from a 58 W fluorescent strip located inside the box which can be changed by lifting the seat.

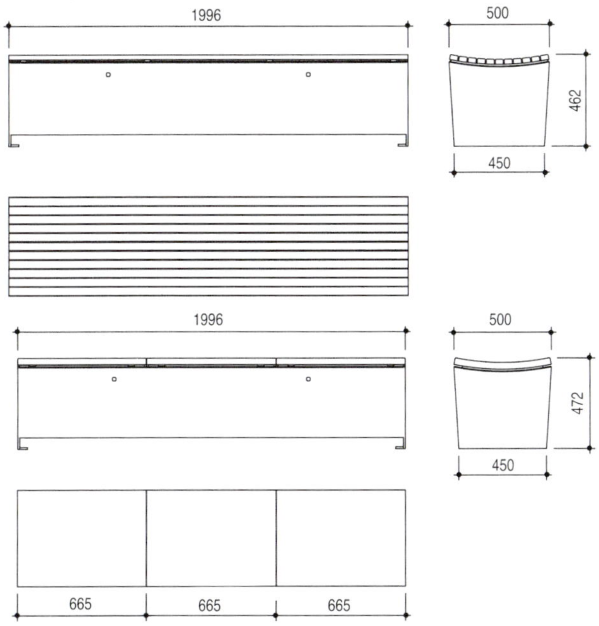

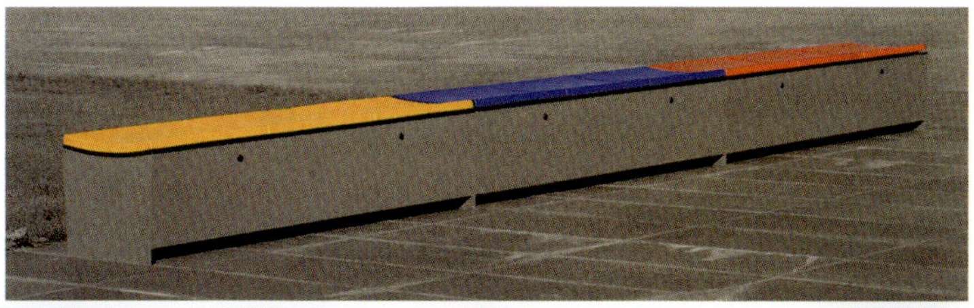

Racional

Design: Franc Fernández Collaborator: Sergio Fernández
Production: Tecam BCN

This modular bench, made of aluminum, has been carefully designed so that it can be combined with other materials such as granite, wood, leather and rubber. This allows it to adapt to any location or urban environment. The main structural element is 50 cm wide, and consists of a single sheet that gradually curves to form the backrest, the seat and the support. The image shows models with wooden seats and backrests, in a group of three modules, including armrests.

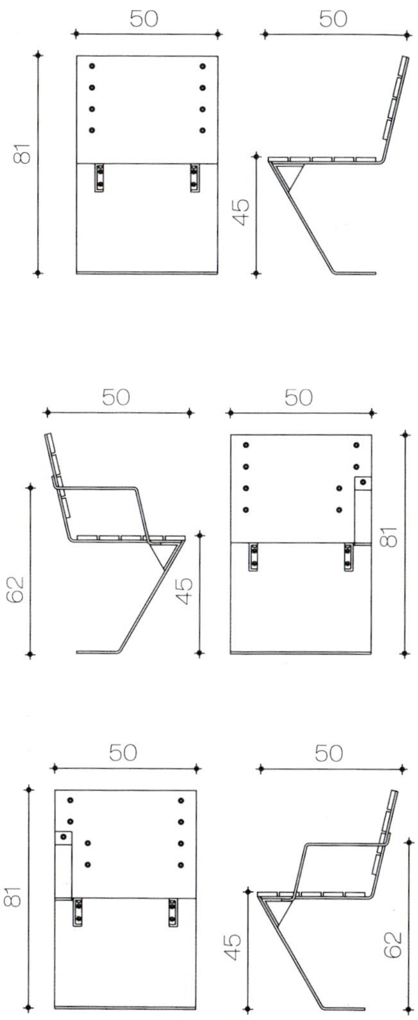
50
50
81
45
50
50
62
45
81
50
50
81
45
62

Mobilia Bench

Design: EBDNBA
Production: GHform

The Mobilia collection is made up of a series of urban elements designed with a view to giving some personality and identity to the spaces where they are installed. The bench that is part of the series can be either straight or curved, thanks to the flexibility which comes from the separations between the wooden slats of the bench seat. The wastepaper basket visible at the end of the curved bench is partly buried in the ground so as to maximize its capacity while minimizing its volume. The materials used in the bench are steel, cast iron and wood. The basic model, measuring 2 m (78.6 inches) in length, 600 mm (23.58 inches) in depth and 460 mm (18.08 inches) in height, can be added to repeatedly until the required length is reached.

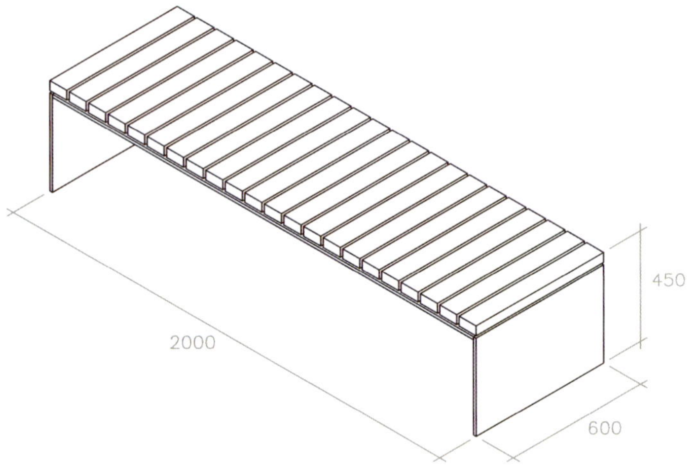

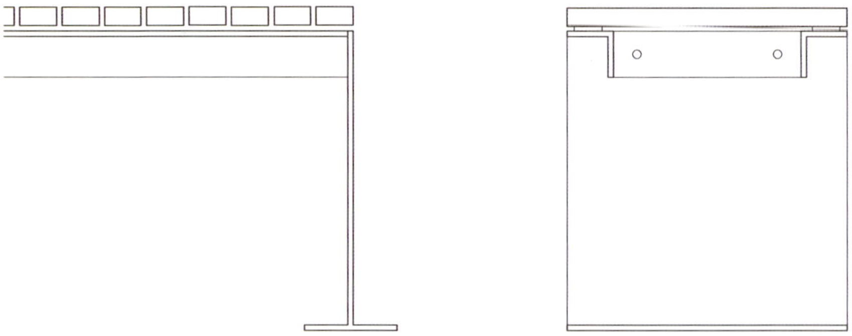

Mingle - Shade

Design: Frog Design Team
Production: Landscape Forms

Mingle is a carousel-style table with attached cantilevered seats that are easy to get in and out of. Asymmetric in shape, it imparts a sense of action and movement. The table surface and the chairs grow out of the same tubular steel supporting structure, an open-ended steel ring attached to the floor. There are two options for the chair components, with or without a backrest. The basic artifact measures 85" in diameter 32" in height. It weighs 75 lbs/per seat.

With the added option of mounting Shade, the sunscreen accessory, this piece of outdoor furniture consists of three functions rolled into one. Polycarbonate is used for the seating surfaces and shade wings. The tabletops are solid surfaces of compression-molded acrylic. All steel parts are primed with E-coat. All painted parts are polyester powdercoated.

Deca

Design: Tobia Repossi
Production: Modo

A relaxing seat like a chaise longue designed for urban parks and gardens. The structure is composed of two simple curved elements, each made out of six Fe 360 B steel tubes bolted together. The ends are fixed in position by a steel plate. The entire item is hot galvanized and powder coated for outdoor use. The structure has two plates at the base with holes for fixing the bench to the ground by means of M10 plugs, suitable for the paving.
The bench is available also in the AISI 304 stainless steel version.
Dimensions:
Height 930 mm.
Depth 440 mm.
Length 1880 mm.

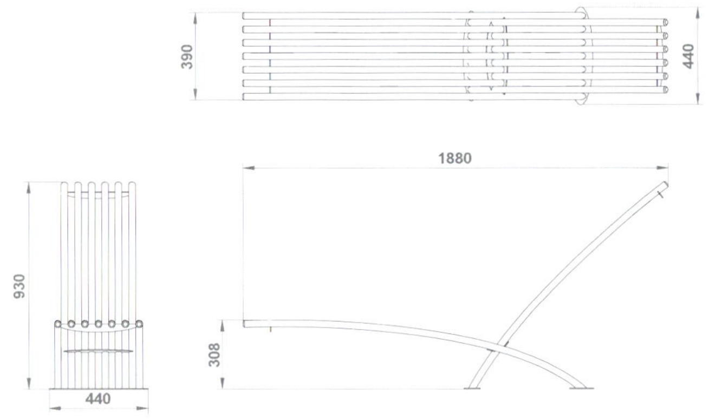

Miriápodo

Design: díez+díez diseño
Production: Tecnología y Diseño Cabanes

Miriápodo is a bench of infinite growth potential, with extraordinarily flexible compositional possibilities. Its articulated connecting system means it can acquire curved or straight lines, turning wide or narrow corners, and incorporating optional items like backrests or arms. This bench resulted from an analysis of the traditional long bench we can find in Central Park, the type used by Jack Lemon as an improvised bed in the movie "The Apartment"; the idea was to create an infinite bench that was not a part of a bigger one.

Miriápodo is formed by equidistant modular bodies joined by a central axis, which is in turn formed of multiple elements, all of them identically constituted and having the same circular movement sequence. The bodies that form the seat can be exchanged at will with others that form the support members; otherwise there is no difference between the two, both consist of a single item.

Solid and firm, yet flexible, Miriapodo adapts and bends to fit any context, like a marvelous example of bio-sculpture. Chameleonic and sculptural, both prop and actor, the elements are made of cast aluminum, best suited for public interiors and controlled exteriors. There is no limit to its extension in length.

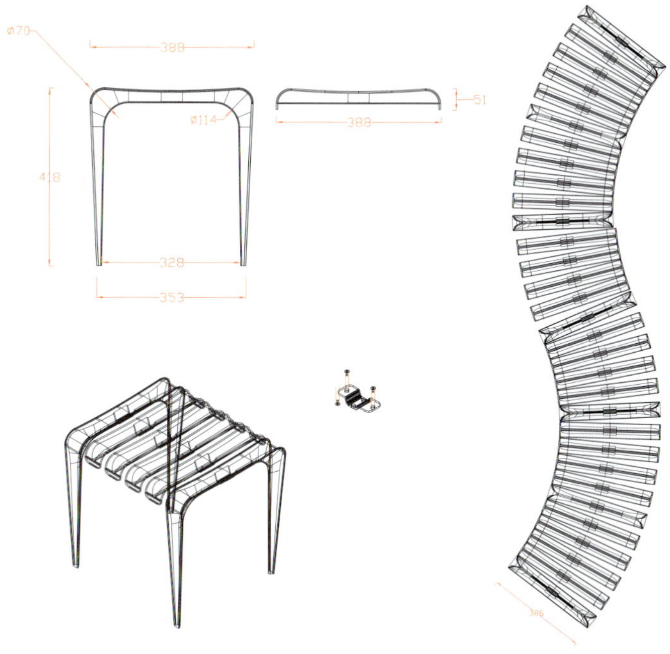

Accesible

Design: Diana Cabeza Collaborators: L. Heine I M. Wolfson
Production: Estudio Cabeza

This urban bench is ideal for resting or reading in a public open space. The different lengths of backrest and seat, along with their constructive independence, allow alternative uses such as a backrest for those sitting on the floor, or lean-to for someone standing or even a protective enclosure for a baby´s pushchair or a wheelchair for the walking-impaired.

The backrest ends as a horizontal surface which can be used to lay out a picnic, as a lean-to for a standing position or as a support for reading material.

Materials

Seat and backrest: solid hardwood, with penetrating sealer, natural finish.

Legs: Cast iron. Finishing: Grit blastined and painted with thermosetting polyester powder coating.

Size

Seat: 2,90 x 0,40 x h=0,405 m

Back: 2,90 x 0,45 x h=0,76 m

Fixing

With chemical or mechanical anchors.

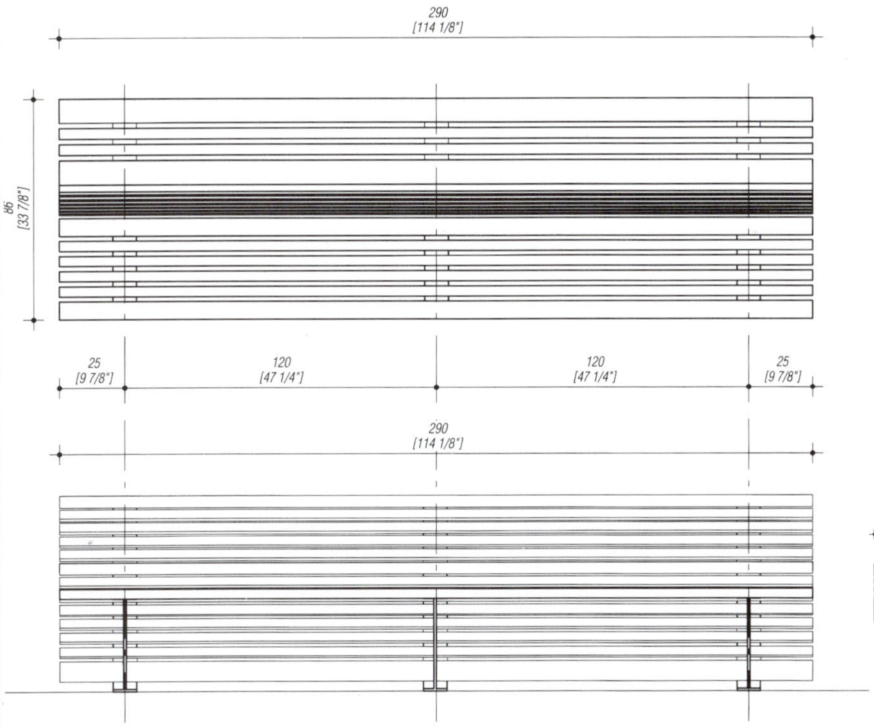
290
[114 1/8"]
86
[33 7/8"]
25
[9 7/8"]
120
[47 1/4"]
120
[47 1/4"]
25
[9 7/8"]
290
[114 1/8"]

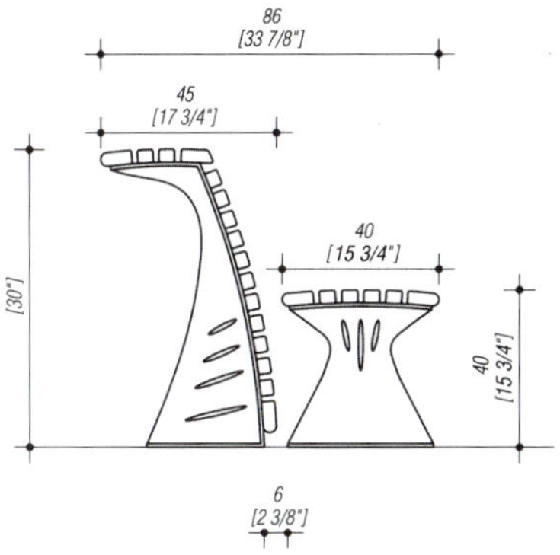
86
[33 7/8"]
45
[17 3/4"]
40
[15 3/4"]
76
[30"]
40
[15 3/4"]
6
[2 3/8"]

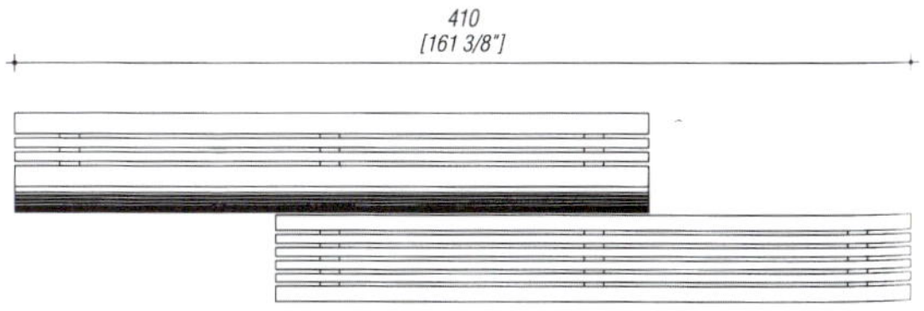
410
[161 3/8"]

Sit

Design: Diego Fortunato
Production: Escofet

Sit is based on the idea that urban furniture should be gentle, round, comfortable and non-identifiable with any particular historical period. It should be a type of object capable of blending naturally into any sort of environment.

The collection consists of two different sizes of rock-benches (or bench-rocks), made of concrete, measuring 240 cm (94.32 inches) and 75 cm (29.47 inches) in length, and 47 cm (18.47 inches) from the ground to the seating surface. The objects rest on a short, invisible rim underneath that anchors them to the ground, while keeping them from resting too firmly upon the earth, maintaining a subtle feeling of lightness, and avoiding the inevitable wobble that would result if the contact surface were a flat plane. Two different sizes of backrest-rocks can be added, making a comfortable and ergonomic piece of urban furniture. The backrest-rocks are held in position by countersunk stainless steel bolts. The different sizes, shapes and colors allow various configurations, enabling the landscape designer to compose his environment in a purely aesthetic manner, which simultaneously fulfills one the spaces requirements, inviting the passer by to sit down and enjoy a moment of relaxation.

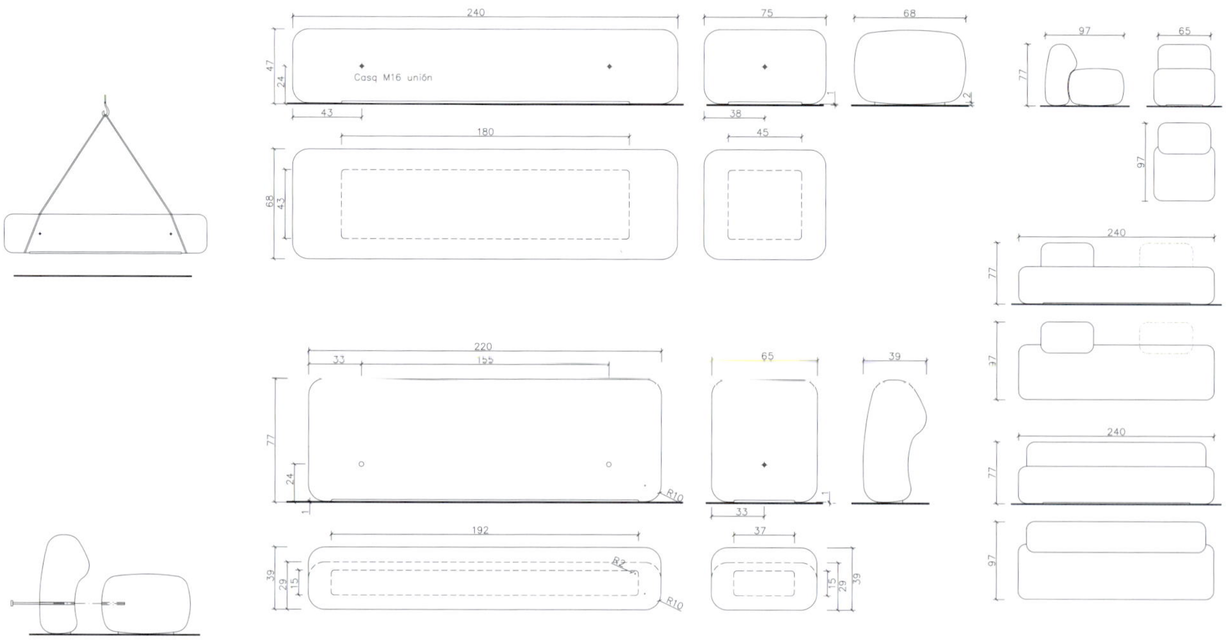

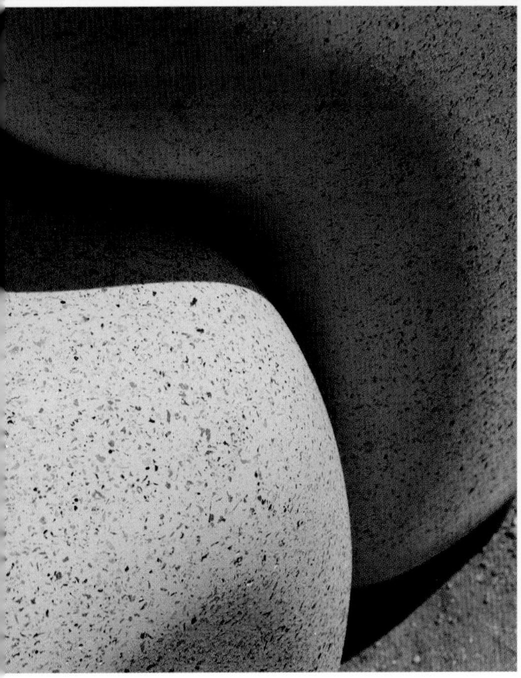

5050

Design: Lisa Segatori
Production: ORA Centurelli

...Why 5050? Because 5050 is harmony and balance, anytime and anywhere. Its line is simple and clear. If you look at it, it amazes you, if you ignore it, it finds you. It joins the concept of emptiness and fullness but also the concept of fullness and emptiness, because 5050 is all and the opposite of all.
It smiles to you and it winks to you, it seems to say "let's do 5050! or better fifty-fifty!". Plasma technology production and much more.
Measures: 50 x 150 x 50 cm.

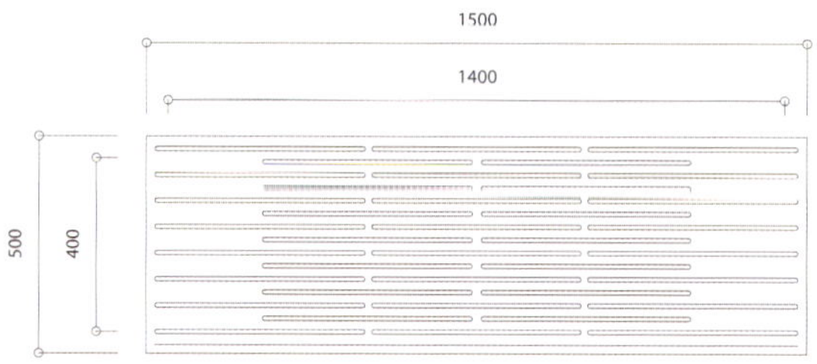

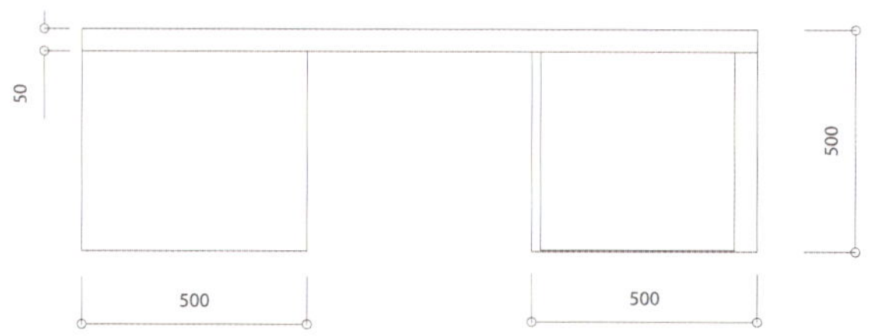

Bloop

Design: Ton Riera Ubía
Production: mago: urban

The Bloop series, designed by Ton Riera Ubía and produced and commercialized by mago: urban, includes four different models. They share the characteristics of functional flexibility and a clearly discernible purity of line, providing a configuration that is easy to integrate in any urban environment, without forgetting the sobriety and elegance that characterise mago: urban.

The configuration of the four models is based on the idea of a bench with orthogonal lines made up of a concrete bench and four A-304 quality stainles stell supports. They differ in whether or not they have a back, located along the whole length of the bench or at one of the ends, as well as a bold pattern on the seat element of one of the models.

Bloop 2m - 220x80x41 cm (86.46 x 31.44 x 16.11 inches)
Bloop 3m - 300x80x41 cm (117.9 x 31.44 x 16.11 inches)
Bloop path - 220x80x41 cm (86.46 x 31.44 x 16.11 inches)
Bloop rest L - 220x80x68 cm (86.46 x 31.44 x 26.72 inches)
Bloop rest C -220x80x68 cm (86.46 x 31.44 x 26.72 inches)

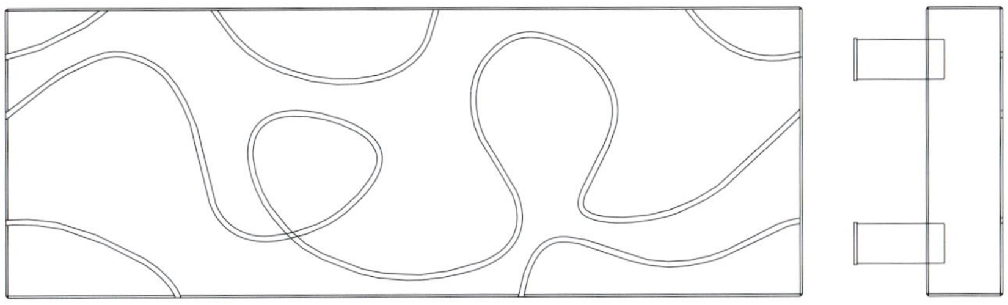

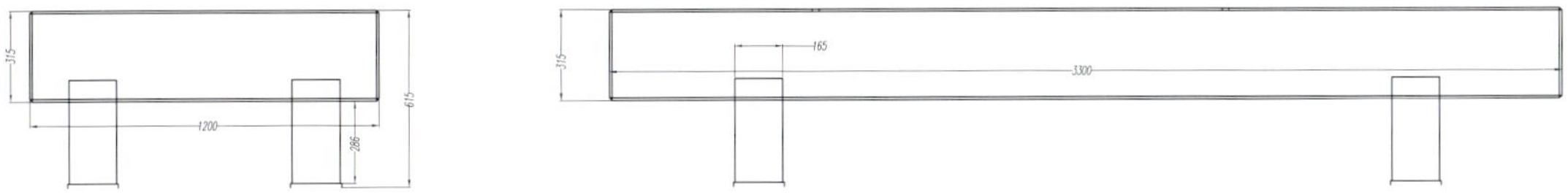

Ambiente

Design: Bernhard Winkler
Production: Euroform

Ambiente Wood – this is the new generation of free-standing wooden benches with optimum seating comfort on ergonomically shaped seating elements. The unique design is convincing in functional terms too – because, despite its refined appearance, Ambiente is extremely stable, robust and long-lasting.
This model is available in wood and expanded metal versions. The metal frame is optimally protected from corrosion by means of a process of hot-dip galvanization followed by an additional powder-coating.
A litter bin has also be designed to match the "Ambiente" park bench.

Cube

Design: Runge Design Team
Production: Runge

With some influence of Far East calmness and concentration, Cube suites public outdoor areas. The pure beauty of the combined elements of granite, stainless steel and premium hardwood is combined with perfect craftsmanship and offers a meditative atmosphere. With its length of 218 cm(85.67 inches) and depth of 60 cm (23.58 inches) it easily offers seating for up to ten people sitting on both sides.

Cube impresses by its simple and clear design combined with selected premium materials.

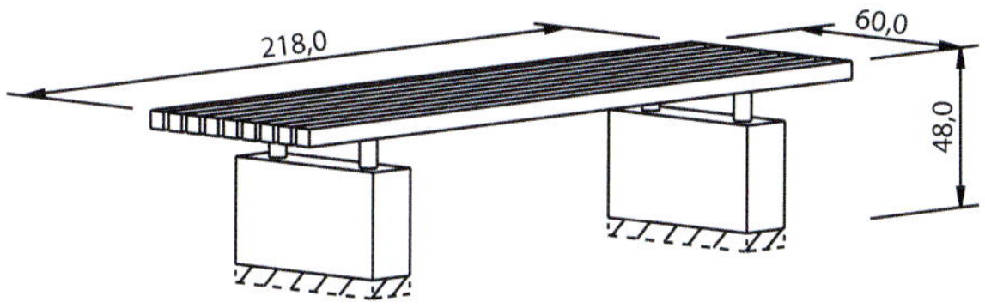

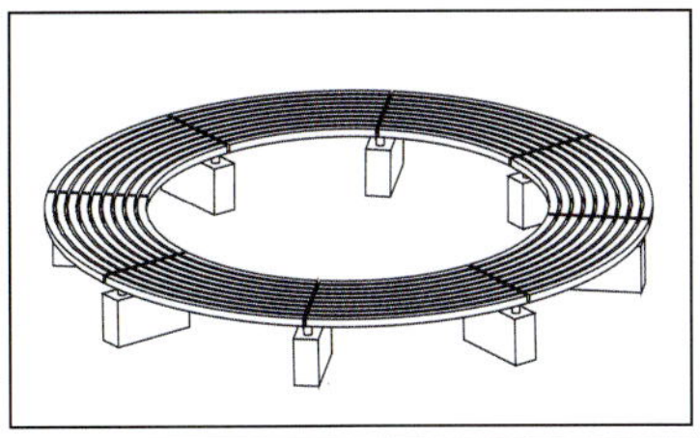

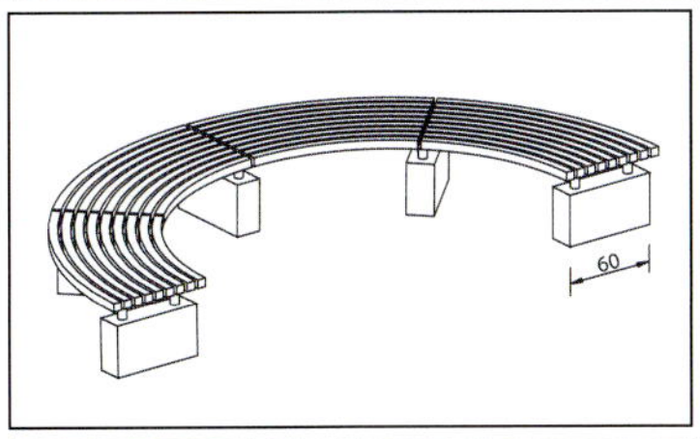

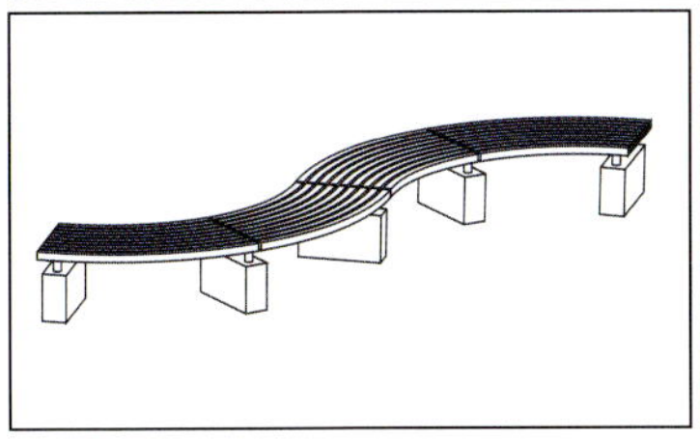

Vera

Design: David Karásek, Radek Hegmon
Production: mmcité

A smart bench presented in a wide range of options shows that advanced modern design does not always mean high price. Durability and toughness goes hand in hand with clean lines and shapes and remarkable lightness. Simply shaped table and park chairs enable to create original combinations in public and private environments.
Galvanized steel frame painted in standard shades. Seat and backrest made of steel round grid, stainless steel round grid or solid wooden boards which are firmly fixed to the supporting frame by concealed screws. All four legs can be easily fixed to the ground.

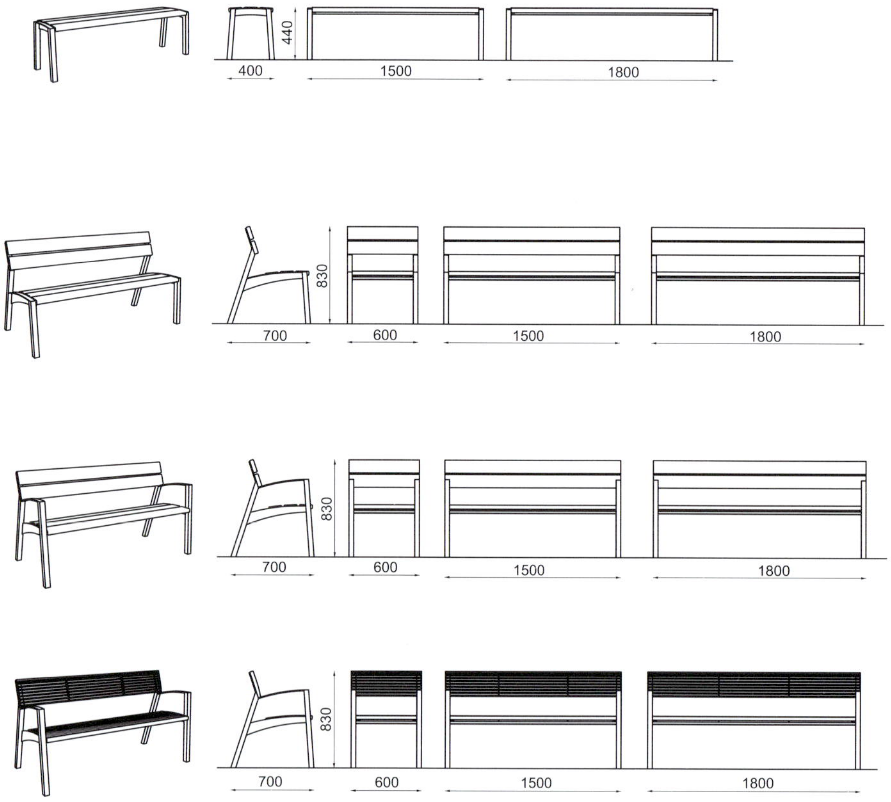

Grindle

Design: Greg Healey
Production: Street and Park Furniture

After Greg Healey's recent trip through South Australia, the design of the Grindle Seat arose as his response to the extraordinary forms, textures and colors of the environment he experienced in the outback. The designer worked in collaboration with Street and Park Furniture to introduce this exciting new range to the market.

Greg Healey established Greg Healey Design in South Australia in 1995. Over time the practice has mainly worked in the realm of urban infrastructure projects with a strong contemporary arts focus. Each work is specifically designed incorporating the site's unique cultural and physical history, focusing on how the work and the materials selected relate to the surroundings on the micro and macro levels. The metal structure of the Grindle seat is of painted cast aluminum with a painted steel sub frame, which supports a seat and backrest of hardwood boards.

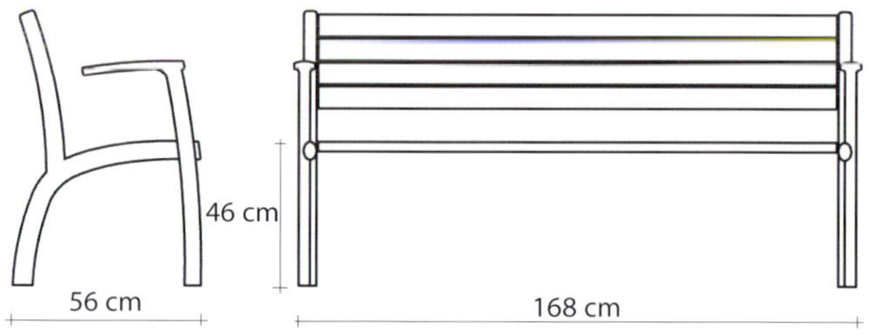

Mobilia Table

Design: EBDNBA
Production: GHform

The Mobilia table provides a functional body, the austerity of which enables it to blend into the most varied urban environments without attracting undue attention, yet without omitting a refined and minimalist aesthetic quality. It interacts particularly harmoniously with other items of the same product range. Mobilia is a series of urban elements designed to underline character and identity in urban spaces. The bench can be supplied in any curved shape. For architectural reasons, the waste basket is partly underground, thereby minimizing its visual impact without reducing its functional capacity. The materials used are steel, cast iron and wood, treated to resist harsh atmospheric conditions. Unity can be achieved by the application of a color, or the basic materials can be allowed to express their physical nature.

Dom

Design: Sergio Fernández
Production: Tecam BCN

The Dom is a simple urban bench made up of five pieces, which include the seat of four 30 mm (1.18 inches) thick planks and two legs of steel tubing, with optional armrests. The planks can be in either Elondo wood or Flemish pine which has been treated in autoclave and given two coats of a waterborne varnish. The legs are galvanized steel, fired with micro textured silver. Stainless steel screws are used to mount the bench.

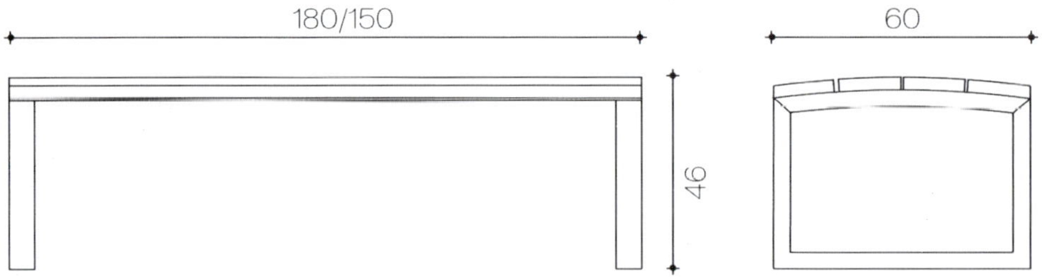

Bilateral

Design: Olga Tarrasó-Julià Espinàs
Production: Santa & Cole

The Bilateral bench is an ergonomically shaped seat that can accommodate a number of people in a row. The optional models with or without a backrest added to its simple and versatile form allows for a number of possible compositions.

The bench consists of the armrests, the support structure, and the wooden slats that provide the surface to sit on. The support structure is made of 6 mm (1/4 inch) folded steel plate, with a corrosion-proof coating and painted black.

The seating surface of the bench, with or without a backrest, is made of slats of tropical wood with an FSC certification and treated with a tannin blocking agent. The various parts of the bench are held together with screws and bolts made of steel with a rust-proof coating.

The article's modular form multiplies the possible combinations it can be installed in.

It is fixed to the pavement by means of two corrosion-proof structural steel screws.

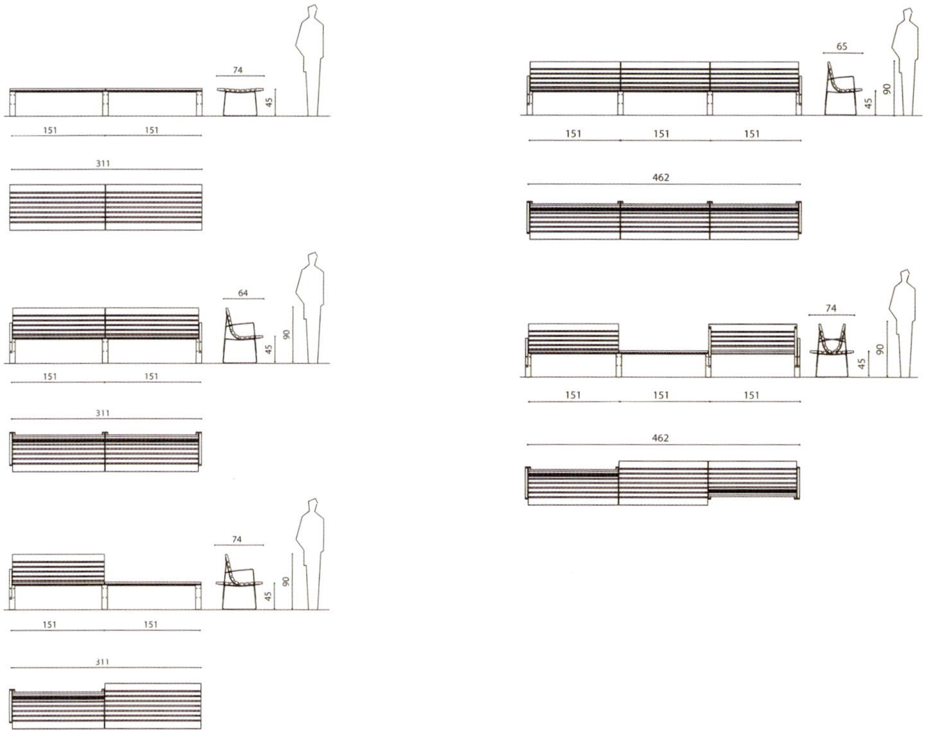

Catalano

Design: Óscar Tusquets Blanca & Lluís Clotet
Production: Bd

One of the few pieces of Spanish design that have never been bettered and which can be expected to remain commercially viable. The secret lies in its well-known virtues. Its ergonomic shape, wisely adapted from the bench antoni Gaudí designed for Güell Park; and the *deployé* steel, which gives it a sense of transparency so that it blends discreetly into its setting, prevents rainwater from collecting and keeps it warm in winter and cool in summer.

"The profile of the bench that Gaudí designed for the Park Güell seemed to us to be unsurpassable, and we decided to adapt it for the Catalano. Done well, plagiarism does not necessarily have to kill the original. The quality of an imitation, as of anything else, depends on the talent of the plagiarist". On the basis of the 1 m (39.3 inches) module benches of any length can be assembled, single or back-to-back, using the type of leg desired.

Materials

Legs in galvanized, hot-dipped or electro-polished stainless steel tube. Bench in *deployé* steel, whith two versions: galvanized and painted in white, or hot dipped.

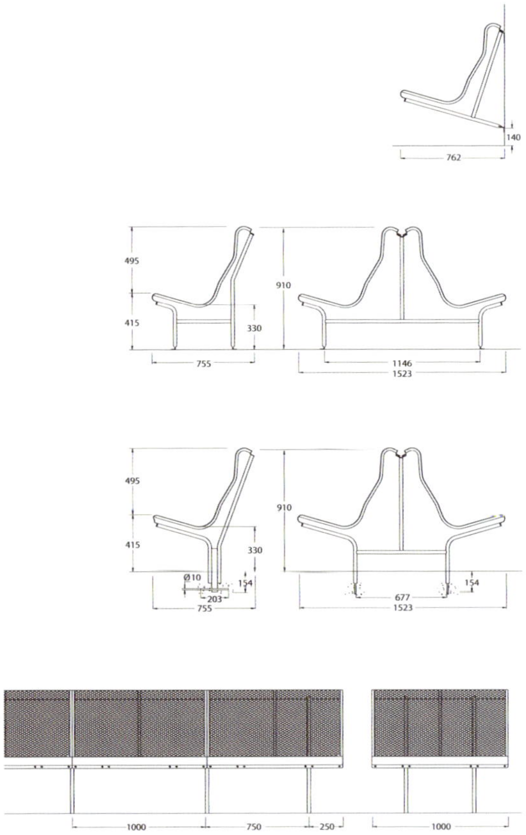

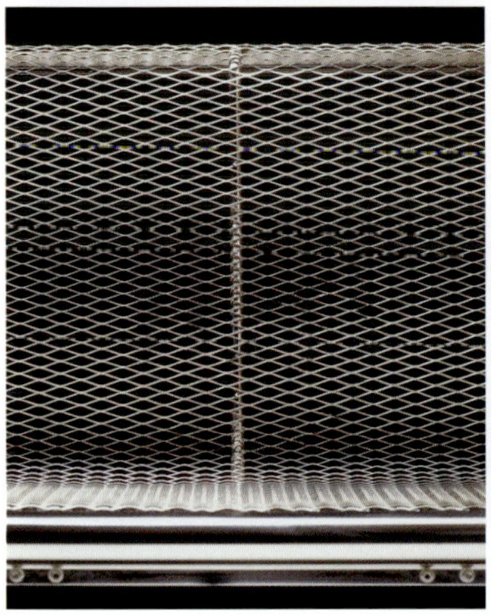

Harmony

Design: Studio Ambrozus
Production: Runge

A characteristic of the Harmony bench, designed by Studio Ambrozus and made by Runge, is the fitting of the wood, which seems to grow out of the cast aluminum, single-piece structure of the feet. The wooden slats are of premium hardwood with a smoothly sanded and varnished surface. A standard range of alternative varnish or paint finishes can be supplied on request. The superior quality of the wood enables it to remain exposed without any surface treatment, UV radiation rapidly providing it with a natural silver patina.

Cornamusa

Design: Diana Cabeza Collaborators: D. D'Andrea / A. Ferrugia
Production: Estudio Cabeza

Cornamusa is the Spanish for a mooring bollard. The idea, the shape and the name of these benches arises from the dockside location they were originally going to be installed. Evoking the stubborn and sturdy image of the rusty old cast-iron bollards that characterized harbor scenery the world over, a reference to the traditional technical vocabulary of the site established.

These industrial looking urban benches consist of a variable and continuous series of prefabricated modules of reinforced concrete with added pigmentation in the mix. The units are linked together by a galvanized steel rod. The smooth finish is provided directly by the casting mold. Installation requires merely placing the items in the desired position upon the ground or the pavement.

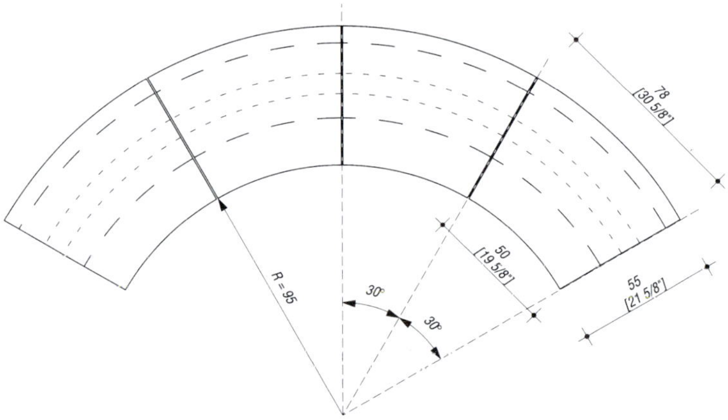

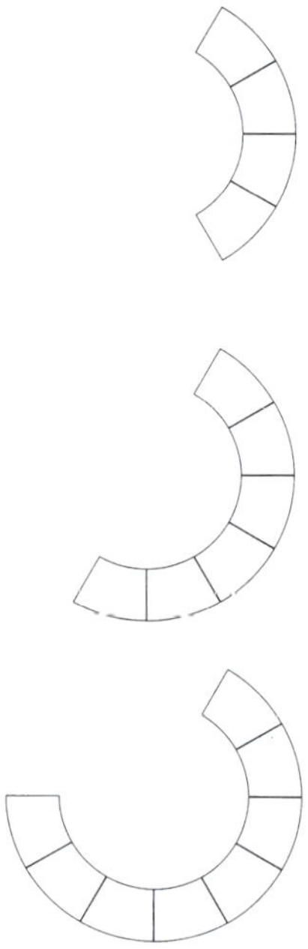

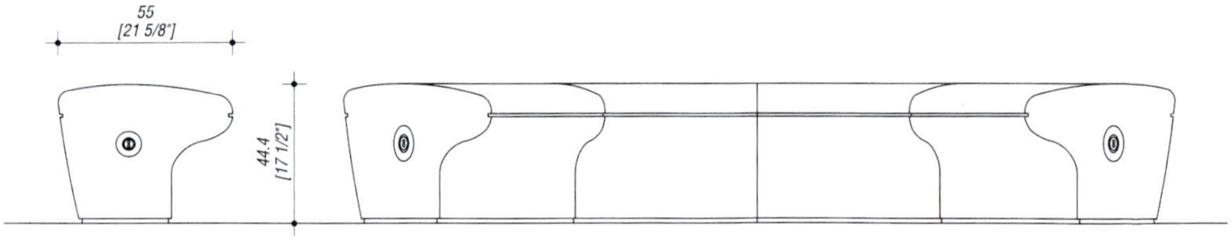

Agi

Design: Lisa Segatori
Production: ORA Centurelli

This product was born as an armchair and became a piece of outdoor seating later. Its elegance is given by the continuity of the frame and its unusual backrest. It is an item that will introduce a harmonious element of design into any kind of ambience, adapting well to natural or artificial scenery.

It is made of electrically welded tubing and tight radium hydraulic curves, with a circular section 42.4 mm (1.66 inches) diameter and a wall thickness of 2.6 mm (0.10 inches). At the base, the tube has holes for the item to be fixed to the ground with stainless steel screws. Three perforated plates welded to the frame allow the wooden seat to be attached with galvanized or stainless steel screws. The seat consists of four autoclave-treated pinewood boards 95 x 45 mm in section (3.75 x 1.76 inches), painted with waterproof varnish. The backrest is a treated and painted wooden pole, 160 mm (6.28 inches) in diameter, fixed to the frame by two perforated welded plates.

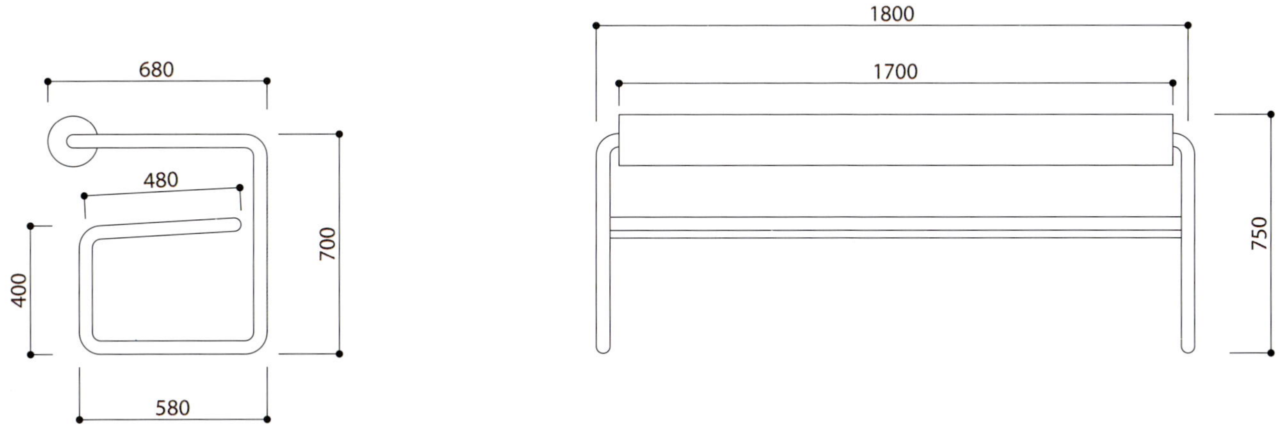

Berlin**Bank**

Design: Thomas Schneider

Thomas Schneider's BerlinBank is an interactive bench for the public space. Its moveable seat of wooden segments can be turned in one direction or the other, depending on the perspective the user chooses to enjoy. The segments of the seat are connected to each other flexibly. By turning over a single segment the neighboring segments follow automatically creating an alternative seat. People can sit next to each other or face opposite directions, involving the user actively in the process of "taking a seat". When not in use, the BerlinBank remains functional in a sculptural way, as the fanning out of the segments creates a dynamic wave-like shape.

In a riverside location people can choose to face the river or away from it, in a park one can watch people on the path or relax looking at nature. Interactive use enables a user to re-experience the location.

Installed along the course of the former Berlin Wall, the BerlinBank allows people to oscillate between Eastern charm and Western architecture. The bench's variability stands for changing Berlin and the communication between the formerly separated sides of the city.

www.berlinbank.net

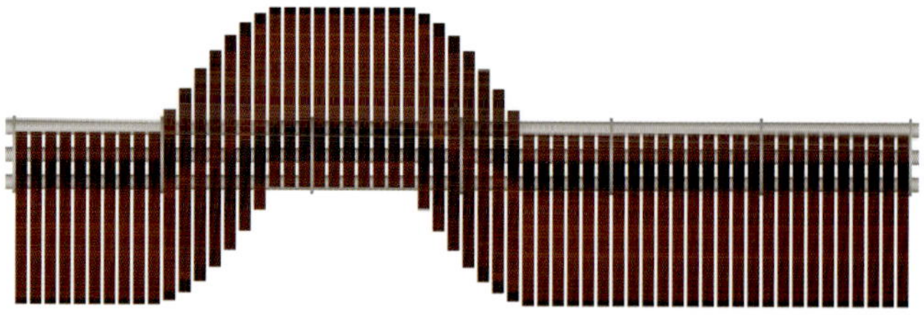

Botanic

Design: Michelle Herbut
Production: Street and Park Furniture

Michelle Herbut, who graduated Bachelor of Industrial Design in 2005, designed the Botanic Bench for a final year University project to suit a specific site in South Australia. Inspired by the growth and organic nature of the plants at the Botanical Gardens, she wanted to simulate the bench 'growing' out of the ground and took advantage of the resulting curve to add another possibility to the ways you make use of the bench, by using it as the much sought backrest that nature so often omits. Street and Park Furniture, with whom Michelle currently works, were approached to help with production and manufacturing issues. With their specialist experience, the enterprise provides urban projects with the convenience of single supply source of street furniture, backed by specialist experience and support. The Botanic Bench consists simply of a series of hardwood boards bolted onto the two curved end pieces made of aluminum.

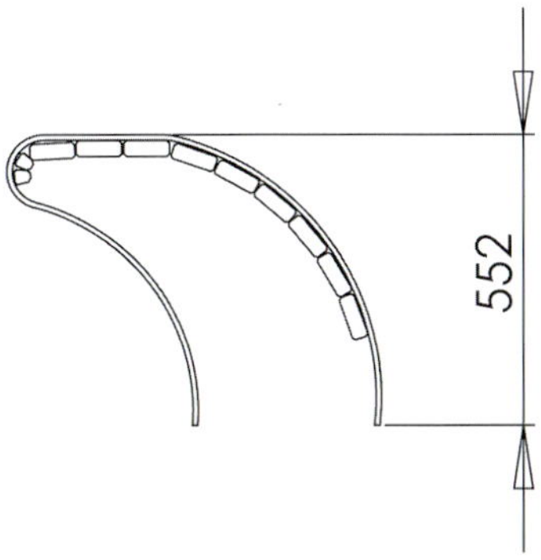

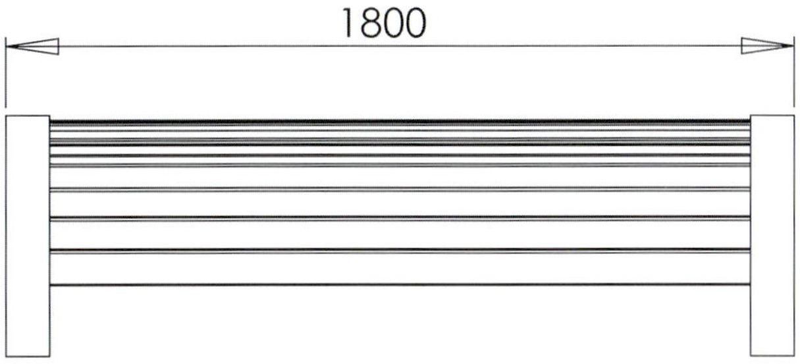

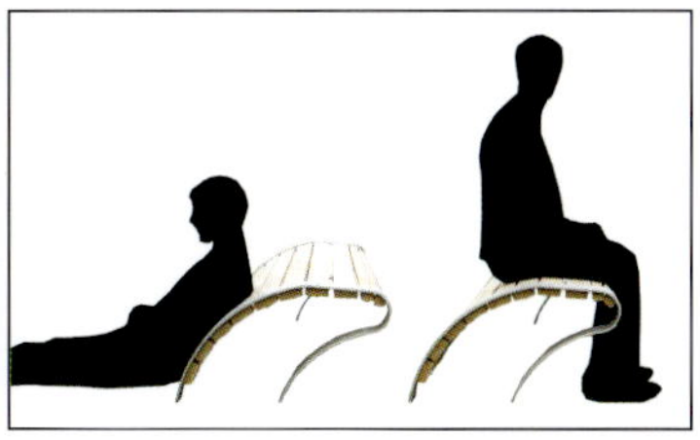

Xurret System

Design: Ábalos & Herreros
Production: Escofet

What do we do in public space? Basically we sit or stand, be still or in motion. If we see it in these terms, a bench is more than just a seat; it's an element that condenses the gaze and motion, an object that demands a form of construction that goes beyond the traditional fundamentals of ergonomics. A bench dictates how we seat and where we look, it doesn't prefigure our behaviour in a definitive way, it stands between us and the landscape ambiguously, with a degree of autonomy from both. This is why it can establish unforeseen dialogues, and seems to be an optimistic and exciting stimulus to create a relationship between the body and the external world. Xurret Sytem is a system for building points of reference, an open combination of five pieces and four colours that tries to trigger different ways of appropriating and activating places.
Main characteristics: A modular urban element, cast in plain concrete with a stripped finish. The Xurret system consists of five elements classified with the letters X, U, RR, E and T, which can form freestyle groups to shape urban or natural landscapes.

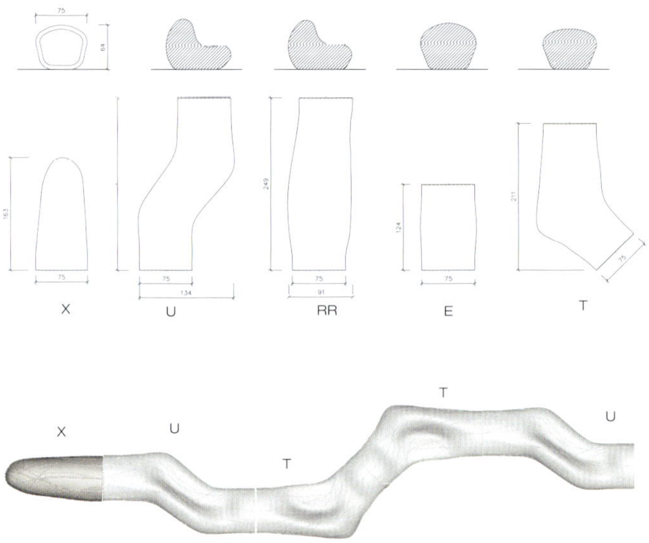

Onda

Design: David Karásek, Radek Hegmon
Production: mmcité

This is an original bench with separate seats, which prevents people from lounging in places where it is not appropriate. Purposeful and beautiful for both indoor and outdoor use, its design has been highly appreciated in the home market and abroad. The arched versions permit various attractive configurations. The Onda range also offers a single seat model which can be fixed onto the wall or a support post.

The structure is made of thick galvanized steel sheet. Separate seats are lightened by slotted linear perforations and fastened to the supporting frame. The range is supplied painted in a standard color.

Onda received the "Excellent Design 2003" award and selected into the Santa and Cole catalogue.

[K-BENCH], [K-BABY]

Design: Charles Kaisin
Production: Vange

[K-BENCH] by Charles Kaisin, is an innovative combination of design and materials. This beehive structured extendable bench allows itself to be shaped according to the user's needs. The poetic of origami blends with modern materials in a perfect mix of tradition and modernity.
[K-BABY], has the same structure and is made of the same material as its big brother, the [K-BENCH]. It is a seat that can be used equally well as a low table. Its small diameter and light weight make it very easy to handle. The K-baby retains a circular shape at all times.

Modular and extendable bench in polypropylene
Material: polypropylene sheets
Dimensions, folded:
[K-BENCH]: 16 x 64,7 x 43 cm (6.28 x 25.42 x 16.89 inches)
[K-BABY]: 43 x 27.5 x 5.5 cm (16.89 x 10.80 x 2.16 inches)
Dimensions unfolded:
[K-BENCH]: 300 x 64,7 x 43 cm (117.9 x 25.42 x 16.89 inches)
[K-BABY]: h 43 cm, Ø 56 cm (16.89 Ø 22 inches)
Use: interior and exterior (UV version)
Colors: white, orange, gray, translucent, fire normative in white. For other colors, a minimum order of 32 pieces is required.
Weight:
[K-BENCH]: 25 kg (57 lb)
[K-BABY]: 5,5 kg (12.54 lb)

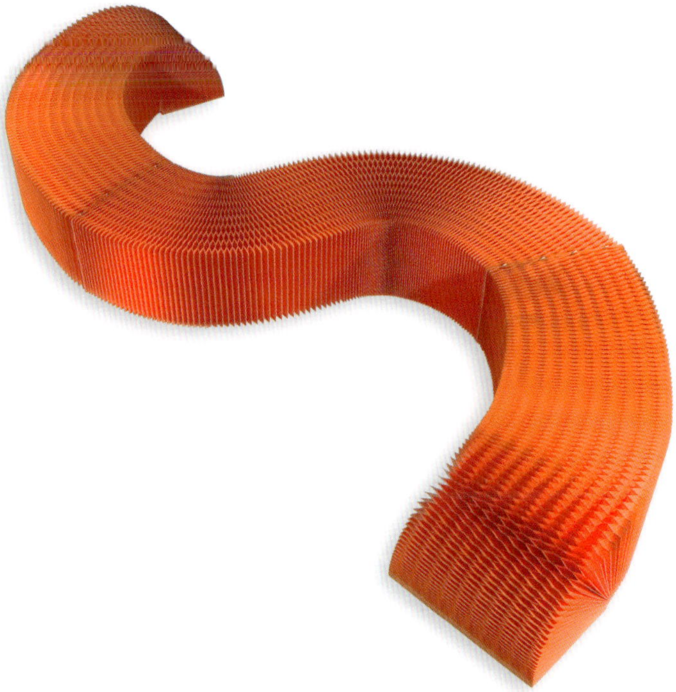

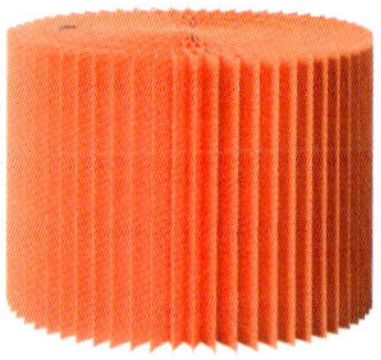

Recte

Design: Ton Riera Ubía
Production: mago: urban

The RECTE is like an everyday sofa that you may find in anyone's home only in this case it happens to be in urban surroundings. It is a piece of furniture for the town which fulfils the objective of making public spaces more comfortable, but does not detract from its elegance and simplicity. The form is based on a slab of concrete with a backrest, two arms at either end and four stainless steel legs. This piece is obviously very tough and made from acid-etched concrete which hardly needs any maintenance. It measures 236x80x69 cm (92.74 x 31.44 x 27.11 inches).

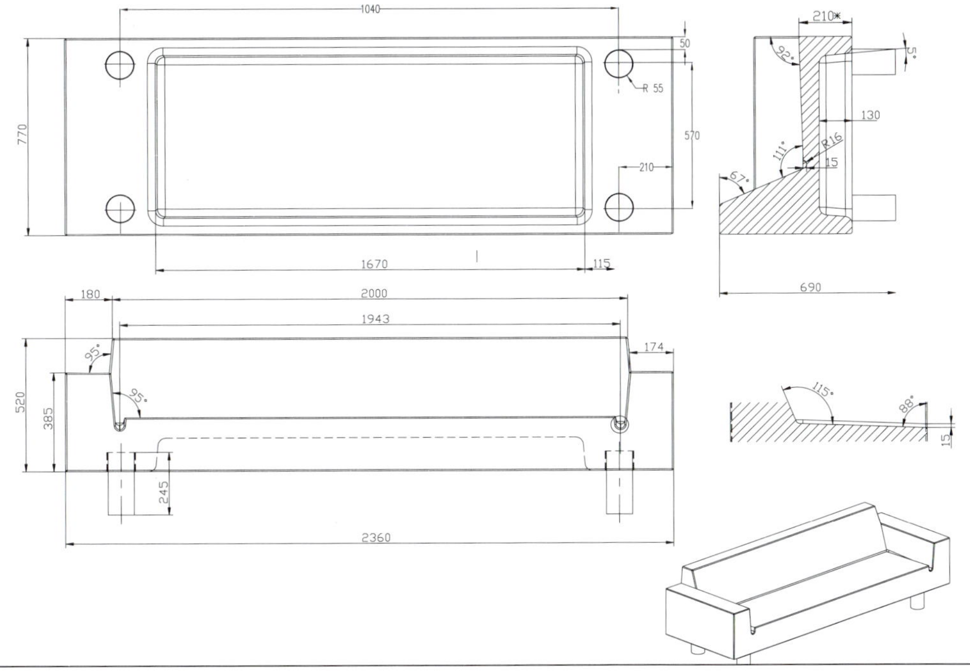

Godot

Design: díez+díez diseño
Production: Escofet

The design of the Godot benches is based on the idea of creating an element of street furniture element that could be integrated into Samuel Beckett's stage-set for the play from which it takes its name.

The bench program consists of three prismatic-shaped elements (single, double and triple), measuring 92, 152 and 212 cm (37.33, 59.73 and 83.31 inches) respectively. These elements are made of concrete and all of them contain a semi-circular hollow at one end. The perforations allow the elements to be placed contiguously, leaving an empty space inside the module that they create when they are joined. This invites Godot to be installed around trees, forming a kind of pedestal that transforms and highlights the trees, while allowing passers-by to rest under the shade they provide.

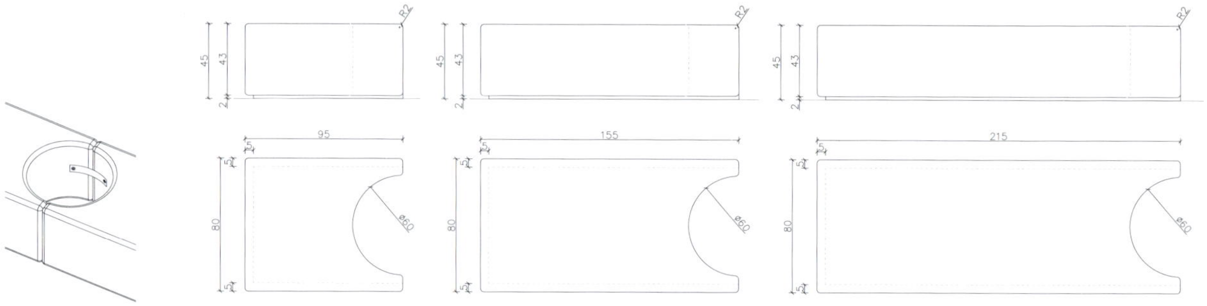

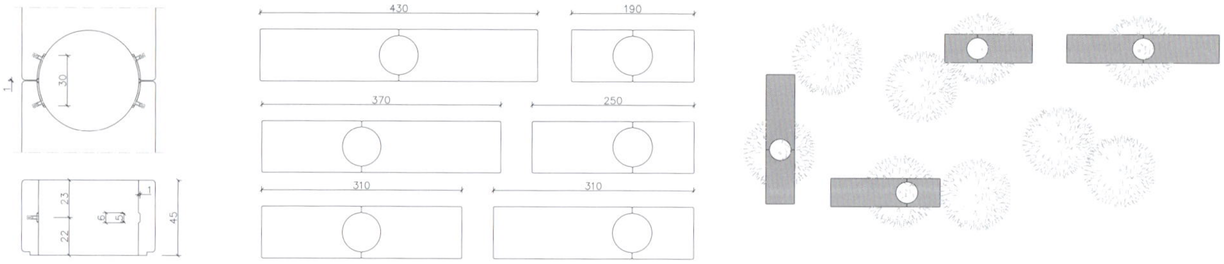

Banda

Design: Diana Cabeza Collaborators: L. Heine I M. Celi
Production: Estudio Cabeza

Due to its robust design, this bench is ideal for low-maintenance or marginal urban areas. The colour aggregate turns the precast concrete into a friendly item that can be used in a number of different contexts.
The system of separate bench and buried base allows to first place the base, execute flooring system around base and level to achieve a perfect fitting. Final placement of bench is then accomplished with a thixotropic adhesive.

Size

Bench with backrest: 110 x 79 x h=42 cm. (43.23 x 31.04 x h=16.50 inches)
Backrest height = 75.4 cm (29.63 inches)
Bench without backrest: 110 x 67 x h=42 cm (43.23 x 26.33 x h=16.50 inches)
Embedding base: 110 x 60 x h=24 cm (43.23 x 23.58 x h=9.43 inches)

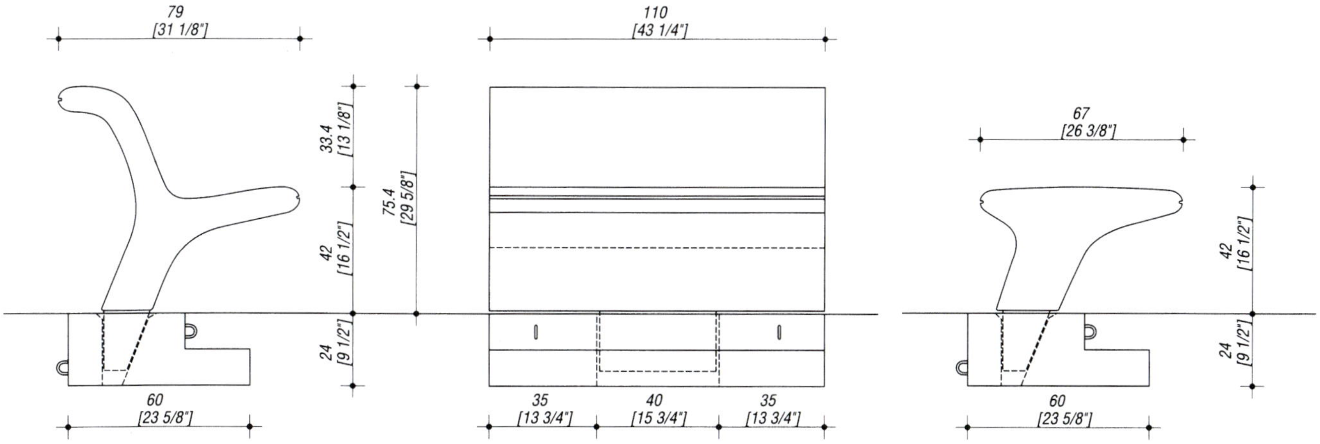

Tens

Design: Sergio Fernández
Production: Tecam BCN

The 'Tens' bench is made of aluminum and autoclave impregnated aleppo pine. The wood comes from sustainable forestry resources. No sort of maintenance is required for its use outdoors, as it has been treated against ultraviolet radiation with acrylic water-born transparent lacquer.

The legs are made of anodized cast aluminum alloy AG3T. The structure is highly resistant. Two wooden boards of 35mm (1.37 inches) thickness provide the backrest and three boards provide the seat. Along the center of the bench runs a curved support member that prevents the boards from twisting or sagging.

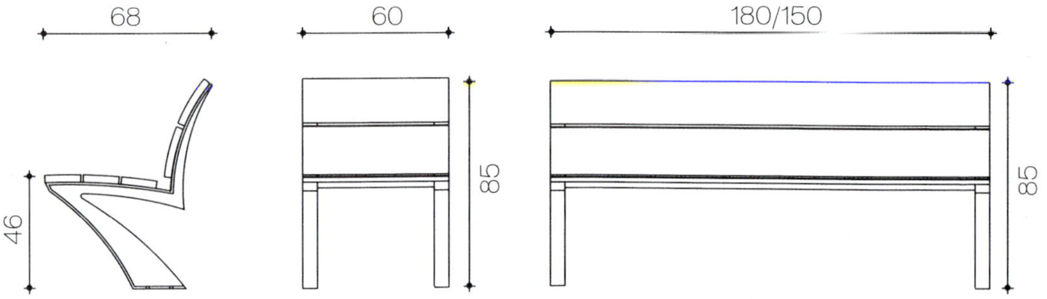

Essen

Design: Franc Dey
Production: Fundició Dúctil Benito

Ensuring that it provides a high level of resistance, the Essen bench is a cast iron seat in a contemporary style. Finished in gray, the mixture of gaps and solid spaces in the backrest and the seat, as well as the purity of its lines, combine to achieve an element that is suitable for all kinds of urban spaces and even interiors.

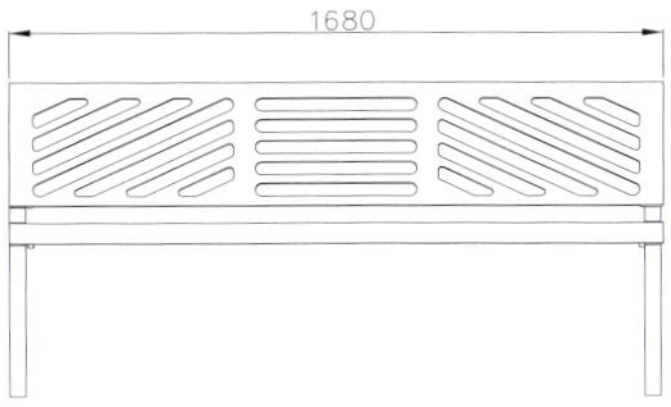

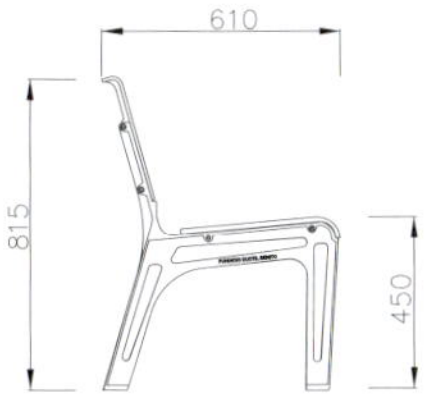

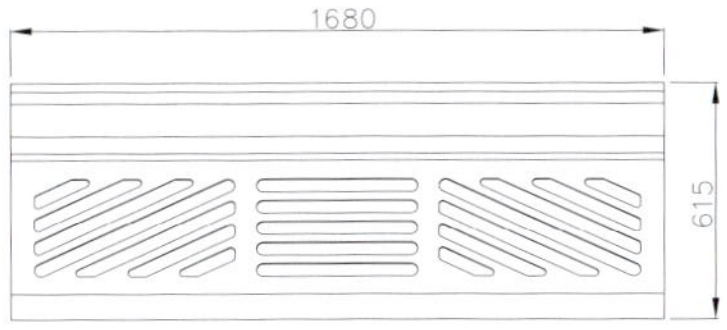

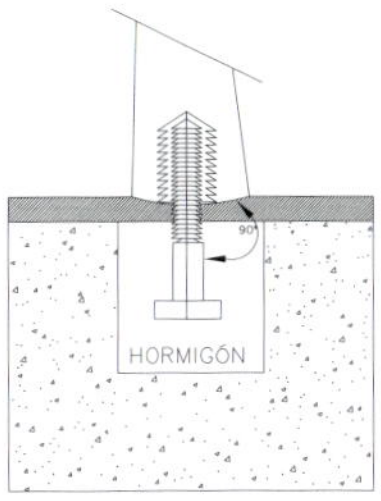

UrbanQuality Design System

Design: Giovanni D'Ambrosio

This urban furniture is a new definition of comfort for people living in the area to which the project is dedicated. The project addresses the needs of tourists walking through Florence and admiring its streets, squares and monuments. The mini components in stone create art events and exhibitions throughout the year, decorations planned for specific subjects which are interchangeable, such as flags, standards, plants and flowers.

These new elements of urban furniture, offer the most attentive tourists a new point of view.

This project maintains a clear view of the architecture and colors of the façades at dawn and sunset, exchanging the standard points of blinding light from above for indirect illumination from light sources close to the ground.

A system of illumination which considers the light bounced off the ground in conjunction with the lights of the shop windows to create visibility and atmosphere while providing tourists with a carpet of light along the places they go through.

The flowerpots have been designed to hold decorations and garlands contained in 'Impruneta' baked vases. 'Impruneta' baked pottery is a symbol of Renaissance Tuscany. These vases will be placed on stilts, exalting the vases from an aesthetic point of view and preserving them from degradation by vandals, preventing the plants from being pulled out and avoiding the vases from being used as wastebaskets.

Wastebaskets will be placed among the urban furnishing, different modules will be used in different ways: as dustbins, ashtrays and hygienic containers for dog's dump.

This project takes into account tourists' daily activities, the unique culture and art of the city and its particular style and architectural vocabulary.

A1. Horizontal basic module
A2. Vertical basic module
B1. Foundation system
C1. Simple break module
C2. Simple break truncated module
C3. Simple break 45º module
D1. Complex break module
D2. Complex break truncated module
D3. Wastebasket
E1. Photos and information module
E2. Display panels
E3. Metal decorative structure
F1. Small fountain
G1. Configuration 1 (angular)
G2. Configuration 2 (linear)
G3. Configuration 3 (specular)

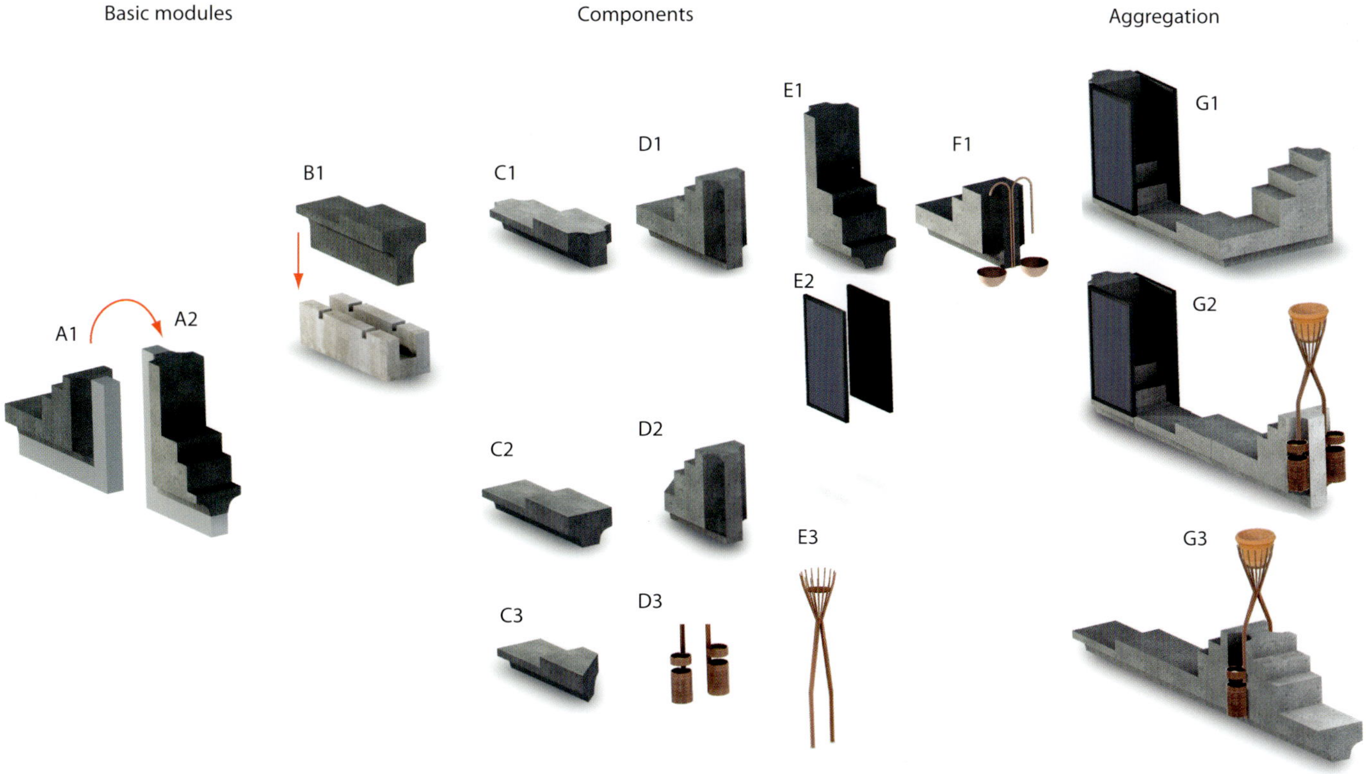

Moon

Design: Enric Batlle-Joan Roig
Production: Santa & Cole

Designed with a young and contemporary outlook, Moon can be used in different ways. The supporting structure connecting the wooden slats to the legs is made of cast iron, powder coated over a layer of rust proofing. The legs are of the same material.

Both the seat and the backrest are made of studs of solid tropical wood with a tannin blocking treatment, 45 x 45 mm (1.77 x 1.77 inches) in cross-section and of variable length, fixed to the frame with stainless steel screws. The back upper "shelf" and frontal "apron" are of 45 x 200 mm (1.76 x 7.86 inch) boards. It is the only bench with a backrest wide enough to sit on comfortably.

The bench is delivered disassembled in two component parts, the support structure and the seat, with or without the backrest. The enclosed assembly instructions are clear and uncomplicated. There are two galvanized bolts per leg, which fit into the previously made holes in the pavement, to be filled in with epoxy resin, quick drying cement or a similar material. No functional maintenance is required except to preserve the original wood color.

The weight of the 1,80m (5.904 ft) bench with backrest is 132 kg (290.92 lb) and 114 kg (251.25 lb) without. The 3,00m (9.84 ft) bench weighs 167 kg (368.06 lb) with a backrest and 131 kg (288.72 lb) without it.

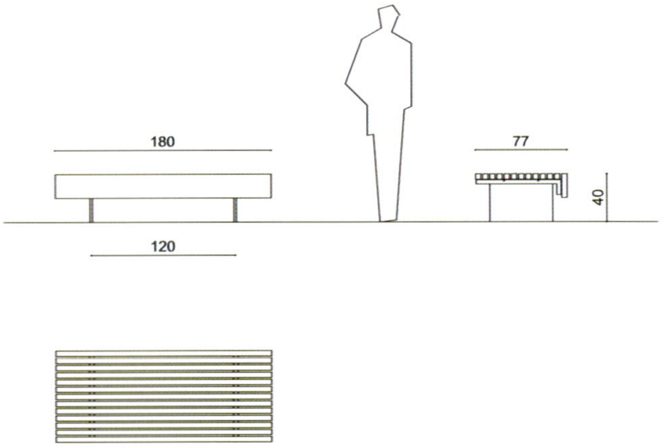

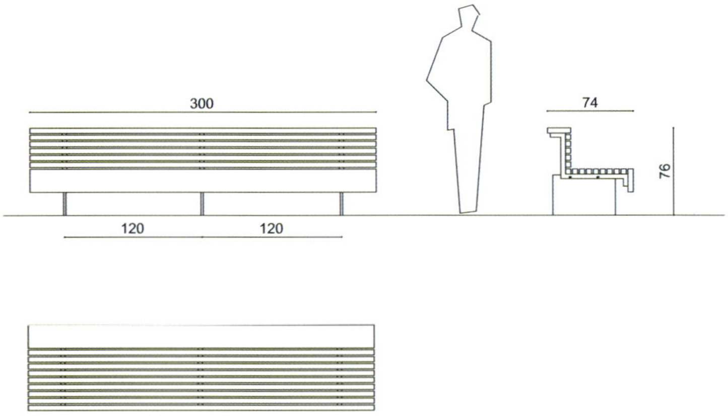

Perforano

Design: Óscar Tusquets Blanca & Lluís Clotet
Production: Bd

"We thought up the Catalano bench years ago, and it has since become a classic of the design of its time, and also one of the most extensively copied projects on the Spanish market. If we are now proposing a new solution, it is not so much to differentiate ourselves from all these poor-quality copies, as to rectify the shortcomings that we have become aware of over so many years of experience."
Óscar Tusquets & Lluís Clotet

The fundamental change consists in replacing the *deployé* with perforated sheet steel. The bench thus loses elasticity and uses more material, but the seat gains a less aggressive texture and is much more resistant to corrosion and vandalism. On the basis of this change in the material, the structure and lenght of the module have also been modified, giving rise to a new handling of the aesthetic.

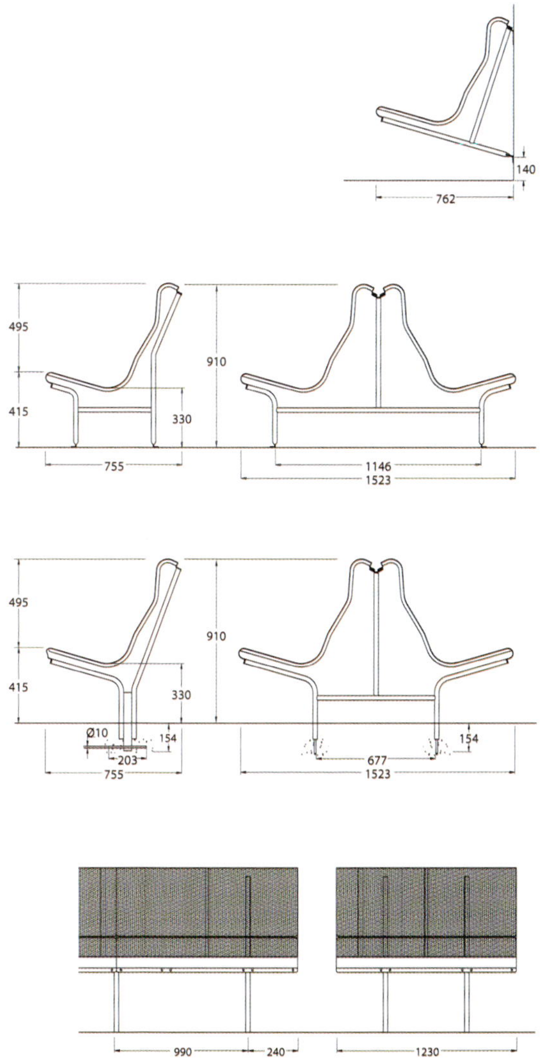

Killy

Design: Ton Riera Ubía
Production: mago: urban

The Killy seat is surprisingly flexible in terms of its functionality, evocative lines and ergonomic capacity.
With the Killy seat, mago : urban offer a seat that has an immediately noticeable purity of line, allowing it to be easily integrated into any urban environment. It won't take the limelight and can contribute to revitalising public space as an experiential space.
However, its main contribution, and the feature that has raised the most interest, is its capacity to transform. The Killy seat can be used as a single unit or in series, with or without a backrest. Without a backrest, its symmetrical action allows it to be used in two directions, as a double seat.
Two kinds of finishes are available, both with excellent thermal behaviour: one uses timber slats, and the other a special wood-resin conglomerate.

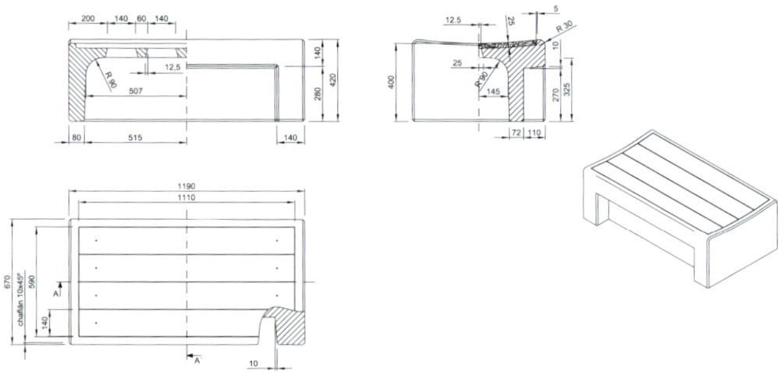

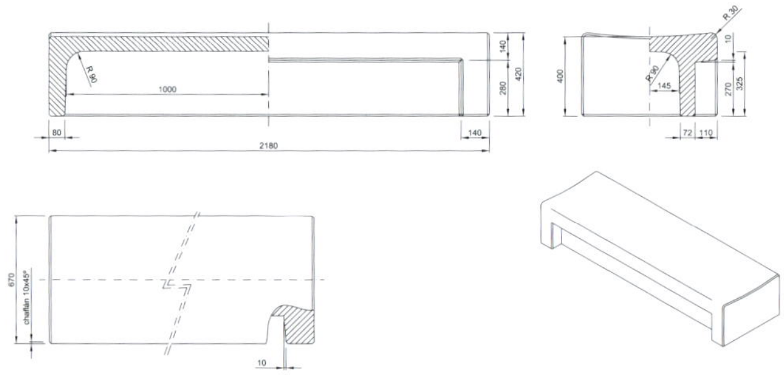

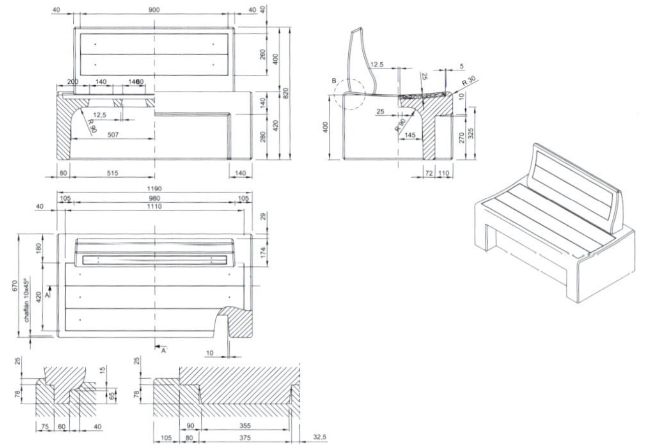

Pillet

Design: Christophe Pillet
Production: JC Decaux

Designed by Pillet and developed by JC Decaux, this bench seats three or four people. The designer has expressed his commitment to creating pieces aimed at groups of people or communities by explaining his belief that street furniture must avoid being bland or monotonous because it contributes to a city's image and is omnipresent in our surroundings. This philosophy is illustrated by the striking but also elegant appearance of this piece, which consists of four stabilised legs, a seat and a backrest. The legs and structure are made of cast iron, while the seat and backrest are made of tropical wood slats.

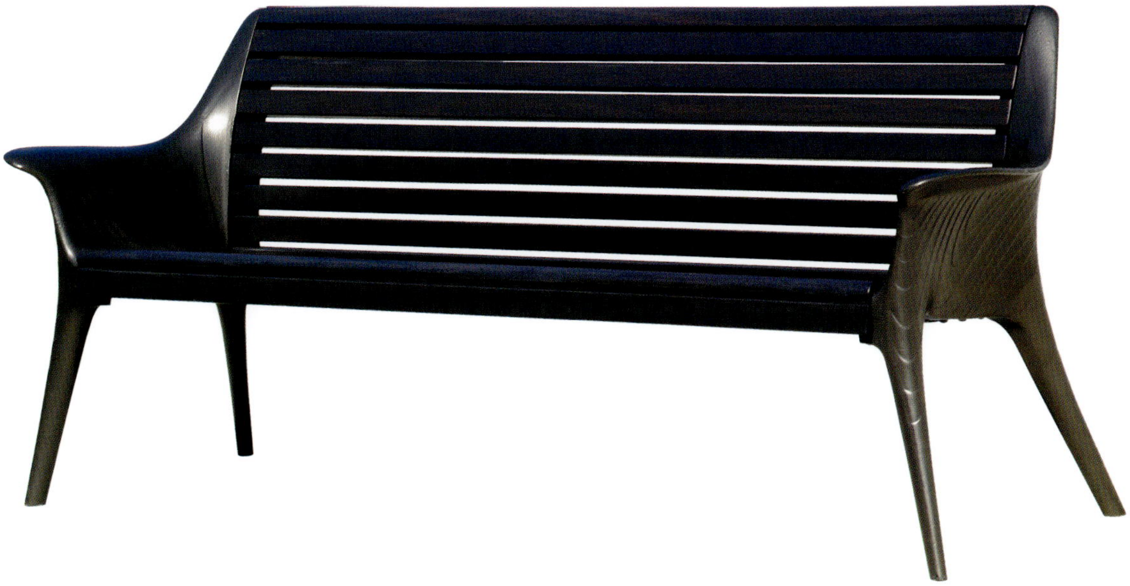

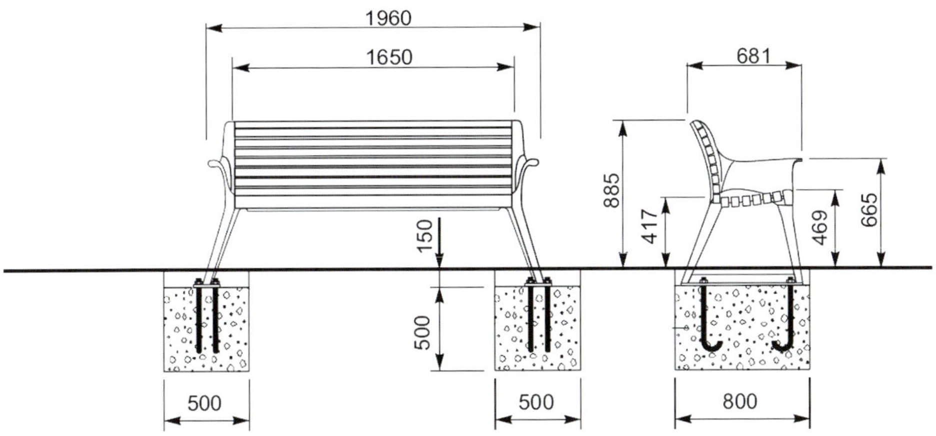

Sillarga

Design: J.Carlos Inés, Gonzalo Milà
Production: Escofet

Sillarga is a reclining chair made of reinforced concrete, constructed in one piece for a variety of use-oriented functional reasons, including its dimensions and weight. Coinciding with the idea of increasingly individualized urban furniture, this item presents itself to the user as a friendly invitation to relax, making the city a softer place. It responds particularly well to the problem of urban furniture in a harsh environment.

Severely punishing climate conditions, vandalism, and the possibility of theft (the item weighs 320 kg) (705.28 lb) are the circumstances this item was designed for. The length of the Sillarga bench allows for a multiplicity of uses. Its friendly shape requires a family and seems to ask for the company of a shorter version, the Sicurta chair.

They are made of reinforced concrete with a waterproofing agent. The object has been treated for the surface texture to show the aggregate (various types of marble). White concrete has been used, to allow for coloring agents to be added. The colors readily available are granite grey, verdigris and beige.

The design of both of these chairs proposes a new manner of using and occupying urban space, changing the rigid linearity of traditional typologies for more open and flexible alternatives, to facilitate spontaneous communicative behavior.

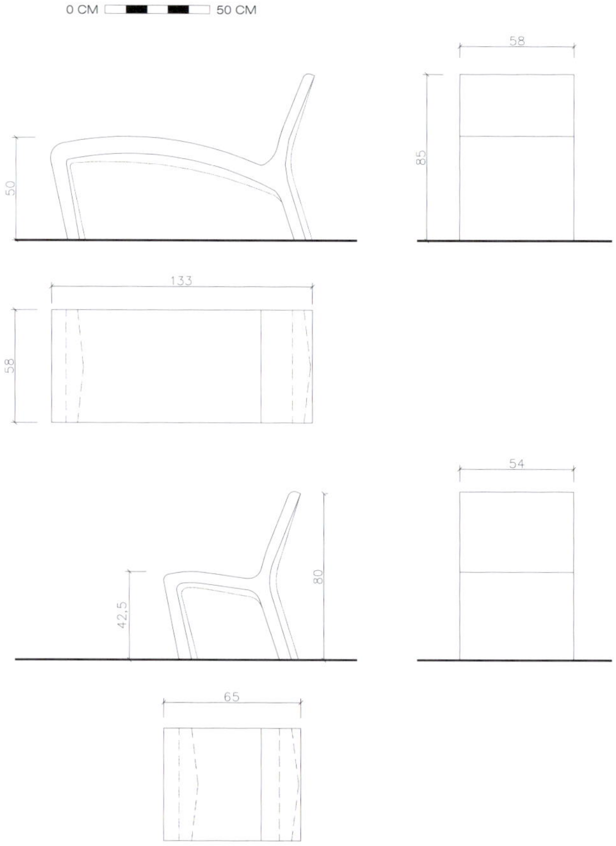

Literas Urbanas

Design: Diana Cabeza
Production: Estudio Cabeza

The intensity of urban life forces us to reformulate the idea of leisure for a better enjoyment of public space, reshaping the traditional park bench and rethinking the concept of seating as an open support system with more neutrality and flexibility.

In this sense, these simple bunks constitute an ideal support for the new uses given to contemporary space and propose, in an ergonomic fashion, different situations: resting with the legs raised, sunbathing, reading, enjoying the scenery, etc.

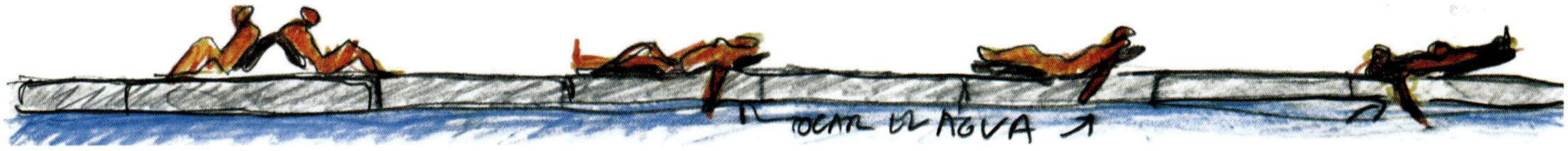

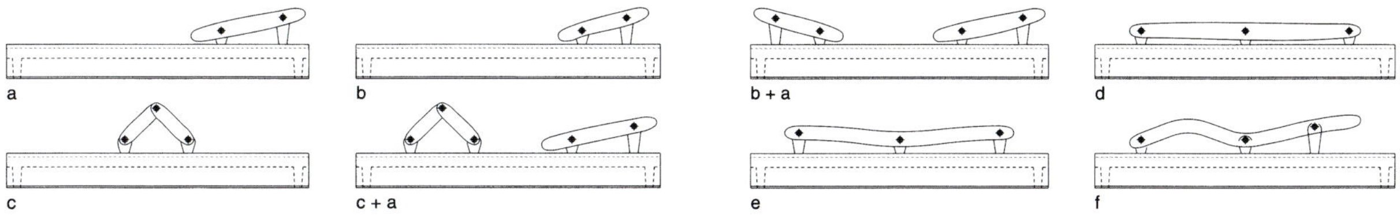

Radium

Design: David Karásek, Radek Hegmon
Production: mmcité

The defining characteristic of this new product line is that its unique contemporary design derives its assets from the aesthetics of bent steel sheet. Optimal rigidity and overall excellent resistance of this steel bench is achieved thanks to the ingenious intersection of its walls. The version with a wooden seat presents a different visual aspect. The seat surface of both optional benches has a rounded longitudinal slot to avoid lounging. The materials used are: galvanized steel sheet for the structure, painted in a standard shade; the seat consists of metal sheet or solid wooden boards (optionally round steel bars can be used). It is provided with an easy anchoring system for fixing to the concrete or pavement. This product line also includes new models of litter bin and bollards. Both of these bench options have the seat sectioned by a round slot to avoid lounging. A small stool extends the possible applications. This product line also includes new models of litter bins and bollards. The series was distinguished with the "Excellent Design 2005" award.

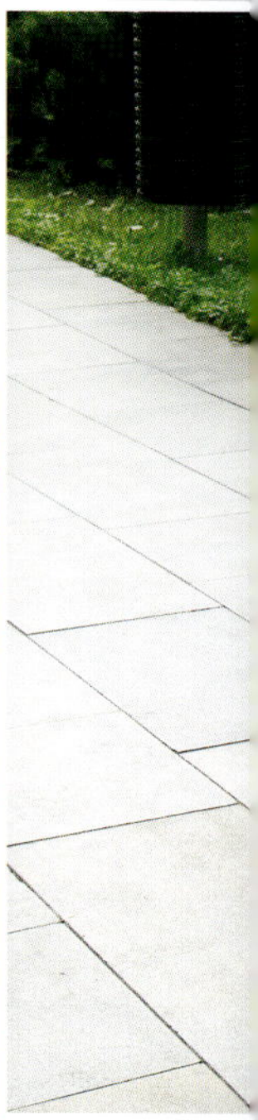

Trapecio

Design: Montse Periel-Antonio Montes
Production: Santa & Cole

This bench is made of two elongated blocks of solid pine wood with a trapezoidal cross-section, which integrate naturally in parks and leisure spots in the city, introducing the formal geometry of a sculptural element that does not immediately bring to mind a bench, thereby facilitating a new reading of the surroundings and offering a multitude of possible uses. The two almost symmetrical bodies the bench consists of are staggered by a 90 cm difference along the longitudinal axis, creating the article's visual interest and opening a choice of exciting ways for Trapecio to enhance a sloping site by underlining its shape. Two 450 cm (176.85 inches) long volumes are made of 20 x 40 cm (7.86 x 15.72 inches) thick structural wooden beams, composed of glued and shaped (lamelée collée) red pine, autoclaved laths. The two blocks are fixed to the supports, which are made of hot-galvanized steel, by means of rust-proof treated steel screws. Trapecio is fixed to the ground by mechanical blocks and two concrete cubes, 10cm (3.93 inches) below grade. No maintenance is required.

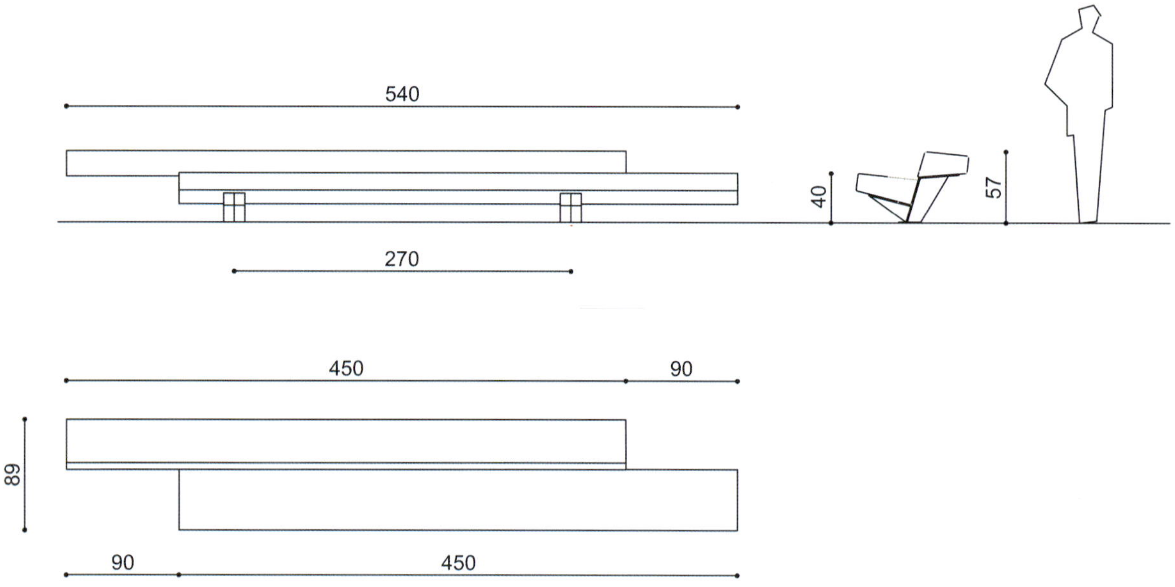

Canapino

Design and Production: Geohide

The notably straightforward appearance of this bench for outdoor spaces enables it to be installed with equal success in a contemporary or a traditional context. Moreover, it has been especially designed to be adjustable to variable grade configurations, by the simple application of readymade steel wedges.

The bench is designed to be fastened onto a stable foundation by whatever type of screws or anchorage system considered most appropriate for the specific location.

The item consists of a stainless steel structure and pipe connections. The seat and backrest are made of ash wood and are easily removable. The entire object is assembled with bolts, making it easy to disassemble for maintenance. The steel surface has a sandblasted finish (natural color for the pipes). The wooden components are treated and painted with a base coat of fungicide and two coats of slightly tinted finish varnish (other finishes can be supplied upon request).

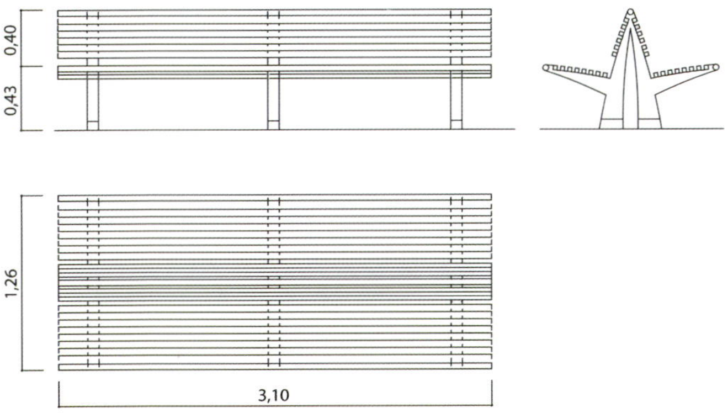

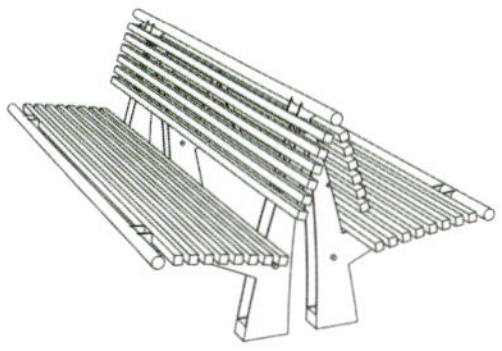

Topográfico

Design: Diana Cabeza Collaborators: Martín Wolfson and Juan José Cano
Production: Estudio Cabeza

Sinuous, assimetrical and irregular, this bench's ondulating surface slides like the earth, glides like wet sand and draws watermarks as on a still damp surface. Its topographic expression evoques subtle ergonomic qualities, and its concrete materiality is user- friendly. Can be configured in numerous and varied ways.

Materials

Precast concrete with color aggregate. Natural finish.

In versions with or without backrest.

Can be matched side-to-side, back-to-back or combinations of both.

Currently available in black and brown and grey.

Fixing

Simply placed or fixed with chemical or mechanical anchors.

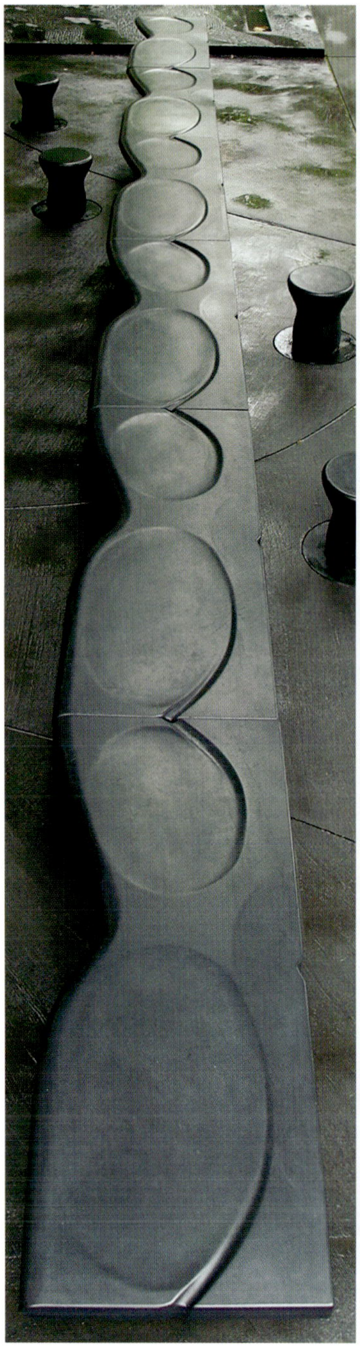

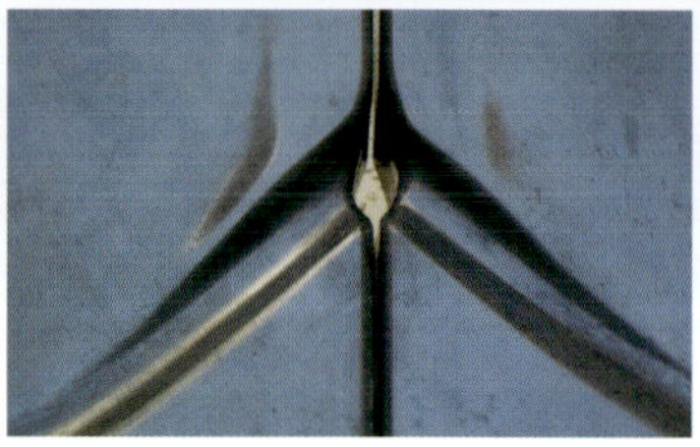

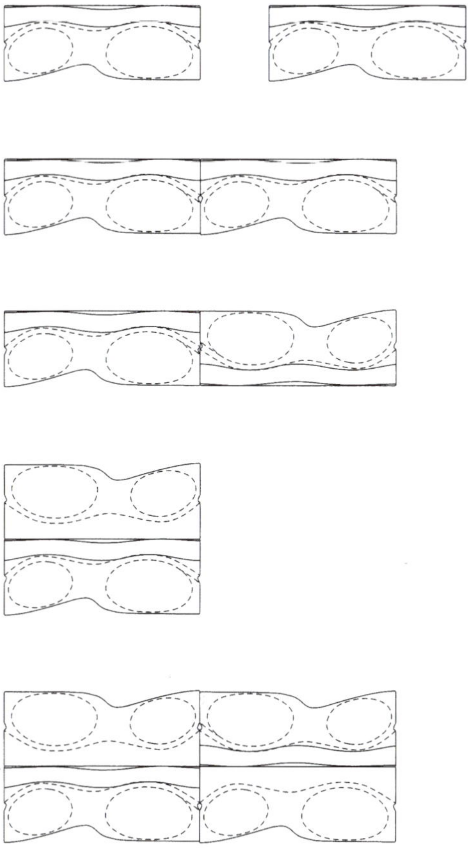

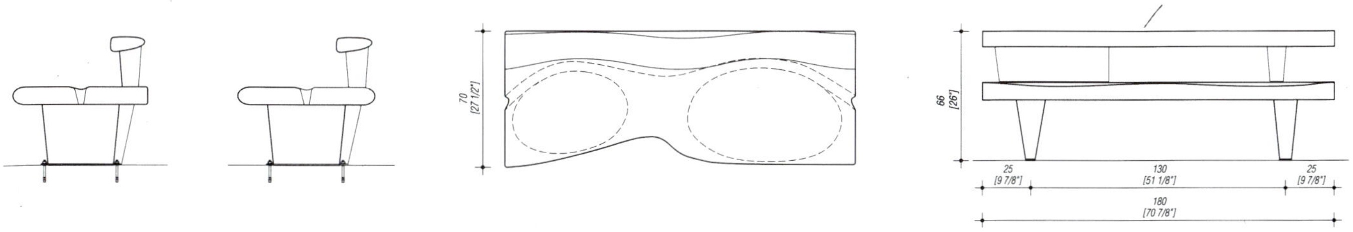
70
[27 1/2"]
66
[26"]
25
[9 7/8"]
130
[51 1/8"]
25
[9 7/8"]
180
[70 7/8"]

Via Augusta

Design: Manel Castellnou
Production: Santa & Cole

An outdoor sofa and an armchair made of wood are an inviting counterpoint to the city's accelerated pace. Its comfortably ergonomic design is an invitation to stop, have a rest, and watch things go by, a respite for the urban inhabitant. The legs and the structural frame sustaining the wooden seat are made of zinc galvanized and oven painted steel angle irons.
The seat and the backrest are made of wooden slats. The armrest is a thicker piece of timber that goes all around the top of the back. All these parts are made of solid, autoclave treated red pine, fixed with stainless steel screws. The weight of the armchair is 42 kg (92.5 lb) and the sofa weighs 73 kg (160.9 lb).

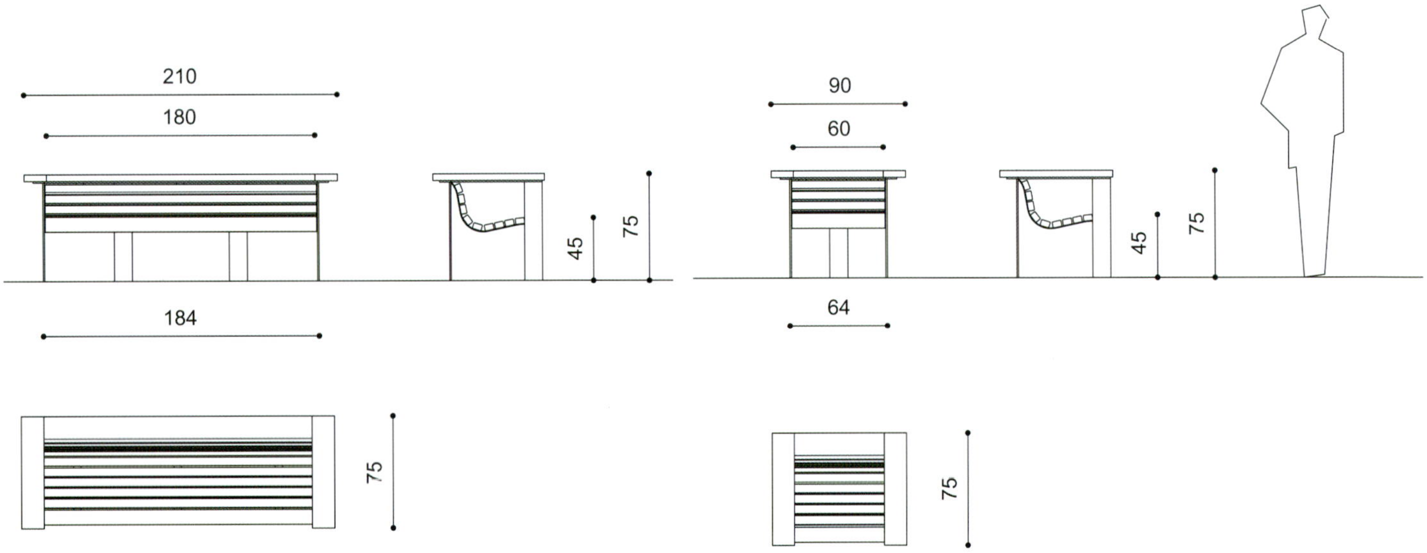

Prat

Design: Mercè Llopis Freixa
Production: Escofet

This design aimed to provide a versatile table and stool set that could be easily integrated into all kinds of public spaces and would be suitable for performing, in an outdoor environment, the kinds of activities that are usually linked to indoor spaces: reading, playing board games, eating, or simply chatting or resting. The table consists of an empty cube, with the only essential parts cut out to allow people to sit opposite each other. The external parts of the cube, which are most likely to be touched, have been polished, and the inner parts have been left raw. The table is made of concrete because of its hardness, ease of maintenance and outstanding capacity to adapt to all kinds of landscapes. It also allows finishes in many kinds of colors, which extends its adaptability to different environments. The table and stool are modular elements that can form larger groups. A second mold provides a symmetrical version of the table, increasing possible configurations.

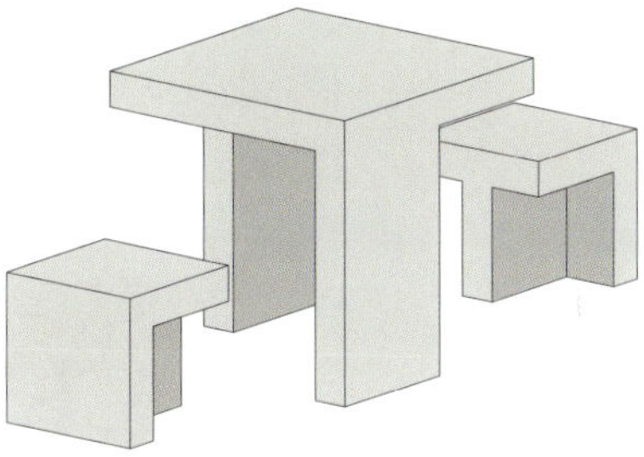

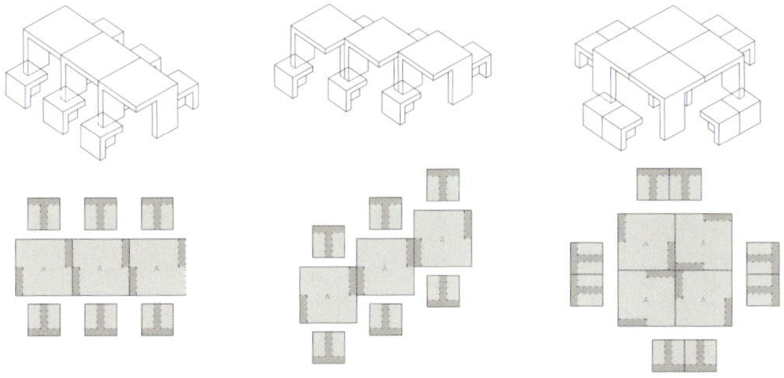

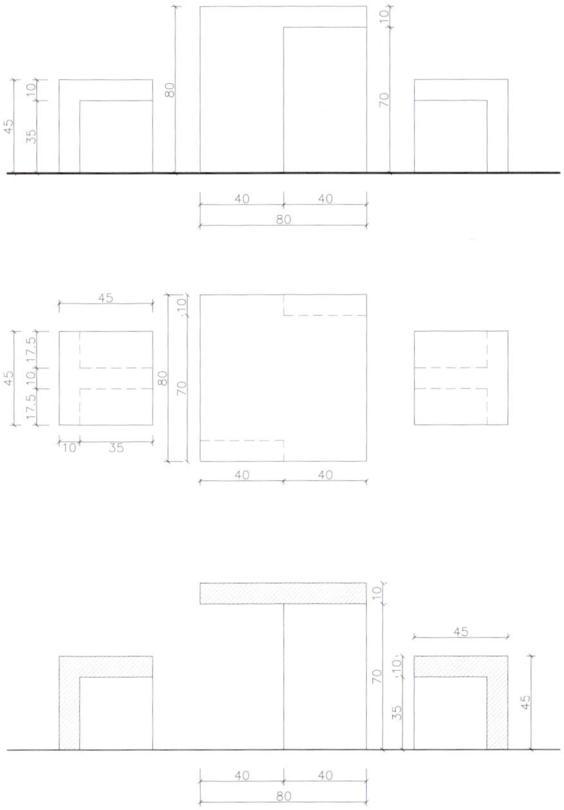

PicNik

Design: Dirk Wynants & Xavier Lust
Production: Extremis

The PicNik is a table-seating combination specially created for the balcony, small surfaces, semi-public spaces, or as an indoors side piece object.
Made from half a standard, massive plate of aluminium (10 mm), PicNik behaves like a 'piece of art', while integrating itself into the surroundings. Outdoors as well as indoors, PicNiks quiet and stylish presence makes it into a real piece of art and elegant garden furniture.

Made out of half a standard sheet of 10 mm thick aluminium, Picnik is extremely durable and provides the perfect answer to harsh outdoor conditions. Chromatising and a powder-coated finish make PicNik almost indestructible even when used in the most public environments. With a range of five standard colors all tastes are catered for.

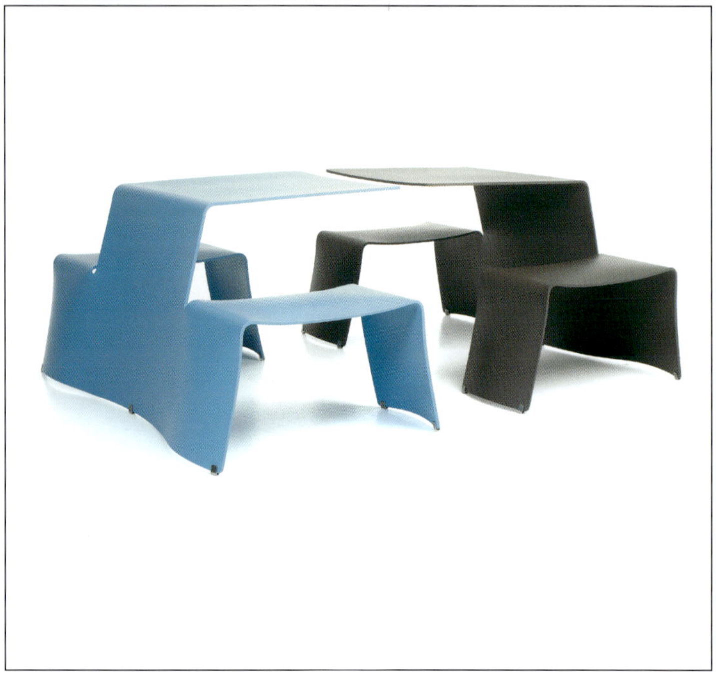

Urban Seat

Design and Production: Botton & Gardiner

This post-mounted version of the well-known Urban Seat by Botton and Gardiner utilizes a cast aluminium frame to support a backrest and seat of hardwood studs. The result is an ideal combination of durable materials, brought together to create a piece of beautiful civic furniture. The Victorian ash wood studs have been treated with Jarrah exterior oil.

The cast aluminum structure and armrests are made of extruded anodized aluminum, which can remain unfinished, powder-coated or polished. The bench has a clearly ergonomic form that can blend into traditional, natural or contemporary contexts. The feet can be made of stainless steel or of powder coated mild steel. Each square base-plate has four perforations for the anchoring screws, which fix it to the pavement.

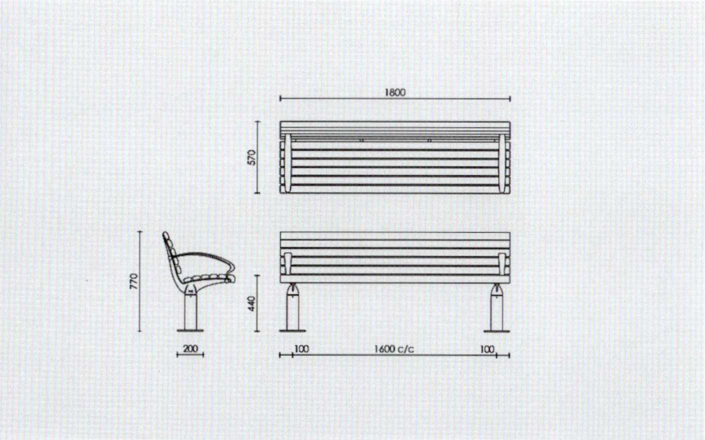

Lungo Mare

Design: Enric Miralles, Benedetta Tagliabue
Production: Escofet

Lungo Mare arose as a result of conversations that took place between Enric Miralles, Benedetta Tagliabue and Emili Farré-Escofet.
For Lungo Mare, the architects wanted a piece that would be as welcoming as a beach and as comfortable as the dunes or the waves of the sea. It is virtually a molded copy, in concrete, of the beach itself. The item looks a bit like a flying carpet. Thus, it will be able to fly to other places, landing in more urban situations, in parks, campus lawns... It took two years to design this item, spent in the workshop and in creative meetings with the technicians in charge of production.
Contemporary landscape is no longer only nature. Artificial objects are equivalent components of a single total landscape. Landscape is the object of a project and all sorts of hybrid forms are imaginable, halfway between nature and fabrication.
Lungo Mare was conceived as an item for public space, a transition between the sea and the beach, materializing the dream of making a metaphor of the waves or the dunes into a meeting place. An artificial space that imitates nature would make opposites meet: representation and abstraction, order and liberty; its shape welcomes the passer-by into the form of a body that is absent.
The item is made of reinforced cast concrete, with a soft surface finish. The stainless steel reinforcing structure is of B 500 S steel, adequately adapted to the structure of the piece, in a quantity of 60 kg per cubic meter of concrete, embedded at a minimum distance from the surface of 2, 5 cm.
The section is undulated and the perimeter is rectangular, measuring 2 x 4 meters (6.56 x 13.12 ft). It is provided with monolithic supports that keep it in a horizontal position.

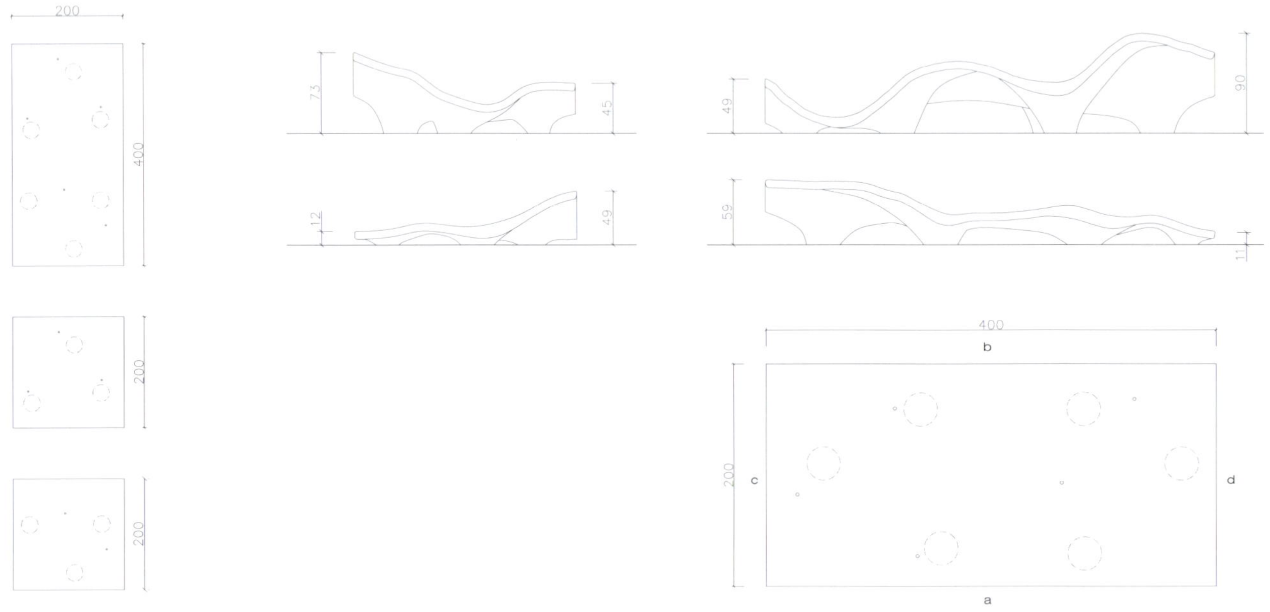

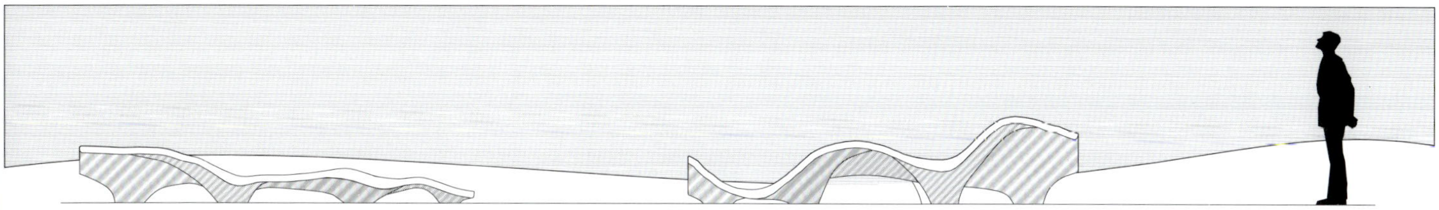

Wastebaskets

Lena

Design: David Karásek, Radek Hegmon
Production: mmcité

The articles from this range demonstrate that the need for large volume litter bins does not necessarily exclude stylish, modern design. The basic structure throughout the series consists of a thick, sheet steel envelope raised above the ground by a tubular leg that offers optimal stability and easy installation even on hillside locations. Its design, structure and optional finishes make this all-purpose litter bin suitable for any environment.

The galvanized steel supporting frame is painted in a standard color. The front comes in four versions: solid wooden lamellae, slotted or perforated galvanized steel sheet or stainless steel sheet. The lateral opening has a lockable door. The item is supplied with stainless steel cigarette extinguisher and ashtray. The inner bin is made of galvanized steel. The item is fixed to a concrete base under the pavement.

Balia

Design and Production: Geohide

In 1992-1995 the city of Lausanne (Switzerland) commissioned Chiché and the architecture and design office Synthèse to refurbish the Place de la Navigation. Given the lack of urban furniture that adequately fitted the brief and the urban context, the designers decided to create a number of items specifically for that project. This led to the consequent design of an entire range of items of urban furniture that addressed the local environment of Lake Leman, with its exquisite views of a landscape and a sky constantly reflected in the surface of the lake, its water birds, and its constant symmetry. Stainless steel is very frequently chosen by this design office, because of this material's durability, versatility, and capacity to mirror the colors of the surroundings, integrating the functionality of Lausanne's urban design into the Swiss city's natural environment. Site specific design is one of Chiche's objectives.

The 45 liter waste basket is easy to assemble, it can adapt to new or existing support poles of various diameters up to a maximum of 33 cm (13 inch). The item measures 35cm x 35 cm in width, has a height of 60 cm (13.75 x 13.75 x 27.51 inches) and weighs 8 kg (17.63 lb) (without the support structure). An aluminum alternative is available, as well as a grey chrome-plated and sprayed version.

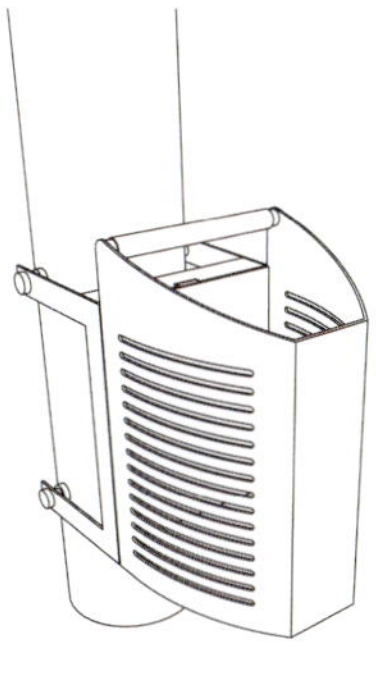

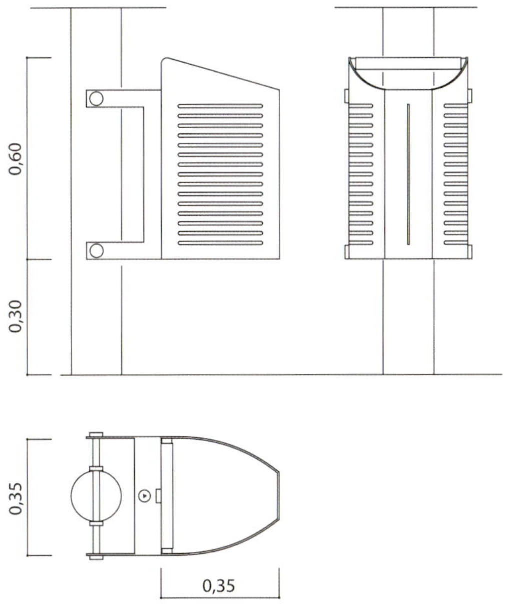

Maya

Design: Antoni Roselló
Production: Santa & Cole

The Maya litter bin is characterized by the way it spans the distance between opposite polarities: transparency and opacity, lightness and sturdiness, functional practicality and a refined aesthetic quality.
The item has a hinged and lockable top made of a stainless steel sheet AISI 304*, with a sand-blasted finish.
The body stands upon three legs and is made of pierced and stretched (deployé) stainless steel sheet mesh AISI 304* with an electro-polished finish. The article can be installed by permanently anchoring the legs into the concrete under the pavement or by simply placing it on the ground in the chosen location.
The self-extinguishing interior bucket is made of black ABS.
The Maya litter bin, which weighs only 20 kg (44.08 lbs), can also be fixed to the ground with structural screws.
If AISI 316 stainless steel is required, ask for prices and deadlines.

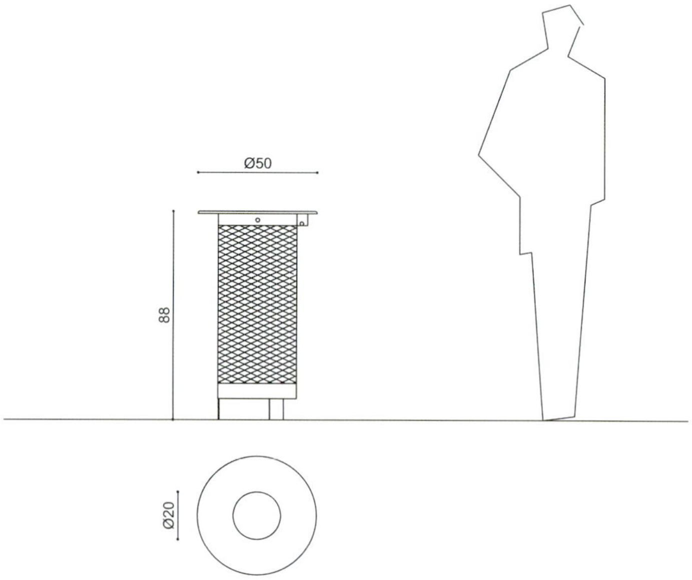

Marte

Design and Production: ORA Centurelli

This item consists of a quadruple litterbin, supported above the ground on the time-tested old square pole. The walls of this item are made of perforated sheet metal, 2 mm thick, with square holes that measure 10 x 10 mm, or a 10mm round hole. The removable lid has an articulated hinge fixed to the pole. Using plasma or laser technology, cutouts through the lid are made in various shapes representing different types of refuse and simplifying differentiated waste collection. The available shapes are bottle, can, paper, battery, medicine, or others. Alternatively, the 3 mm thick sheet metal lid can be left entirely closed.
The 350 x 350 mm base-plate is perforated to take the anchoring bolts that will fix the item to the pavement. Hot-dip-galvanizing is available on request, according to UNI regulations. A choice of RAL paint coating can also be provided.The entire object measures 580 x 580 x 1020 (height) mm (22.80 x 22.80 x 40(height) inches. Each separate bin is 520 x 225 x 500 mm.

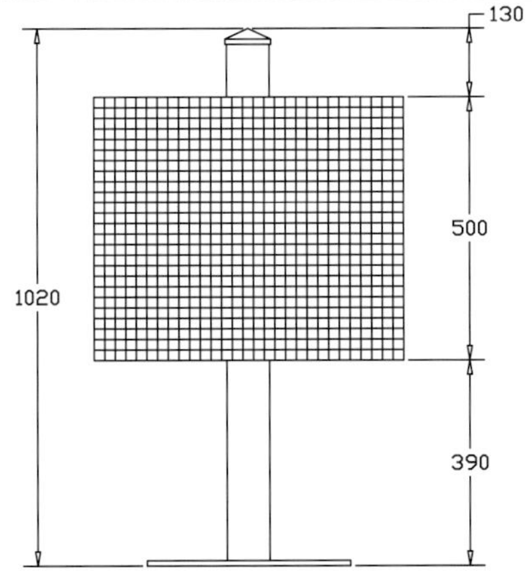

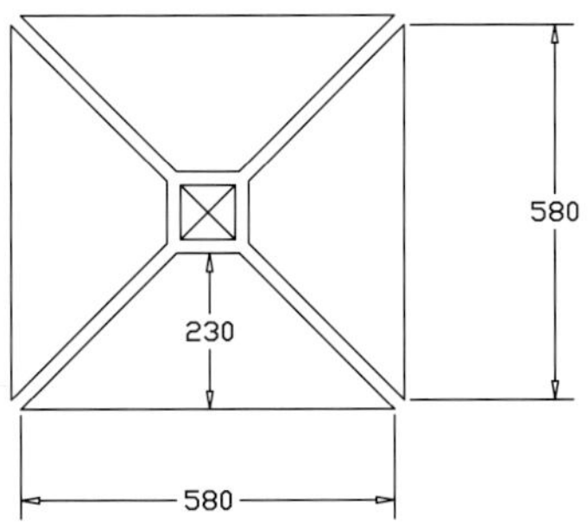

Radium

Design: David Karásek, Radek Hegmon
Production: mmcité

The Radium litter bin is a geometrically styled body with softly rounded edges that is the direct result of the technology of bent steel sheet. The support structure is a rectangular ring with rounded edges that carries the inserted box, which in turn contains the galvanized steel inner bin. The complete piece is an elegant and durable example of a public litter bin. Its design establishes an associative link with the Radium benches and bollards.
The supporting frame is made of galvanized steel, with a rust-proof covering and painted in a standard shade. There is a forward opening lockable door and an ashtray with a stainless steel cigarette extinguisher integrated into the piece's top cover. The item is designed to be fixed to a concrete base or the pavement by means of stainless steel anchoring bolts.

Cube

Design: Studio Ambrozus
Production: Runge

The two colors of this litterbin are characteristic of the design of studio Ambrozus. The combination of a plinth-like base, stainless steel side and top panels and a powder coated front and back add to the item's visual profile. The entire bin is made of stainless steel but the sides most exposed to wear are sandblasted and powder-coated. Stainless steel litterbins are seldom perfectly clean, and acquire a shabby, dirty look, especially the areas at the base and around the opening, which are exposed to more erosion and dirt. Smears are less visible on the powder-coated front than on an impeccable surface of stainless steel. Cube contains 80 liters of easy-to-empty capacity in the form of a lightweight plastic inner container or a plastic bag. Moreover, cube provides a large ashtray integrated into the design, which is pleasingly clear-cut and architectural, underlining its efficient functionality.

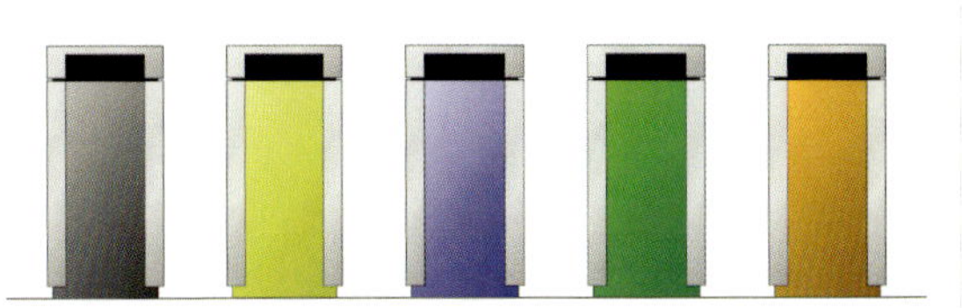

Urbana

Design: Cristian Cirici
Production: Bd

Making good use of these obstacles found scattered along our street represents a challenge: *"Our pavements are full of obstacles which are nevertheless necessary to provide the services we demand: lampposts to illuminate the streets, traffic lights... In view of the high number of obstacles already on the pavements the idea was to take advantage of these inevitable elements by using them as a support. To a certain degree this waste bin is rather like a parasite of these numerous urban obstacles. That is why the bin's fixture element comes in a wide variety of forms, with the only common feature being that no support of its own is required".* Fastening to the wall, lamppost and other urban furniture with Hälfen. To the floor with a built in support.

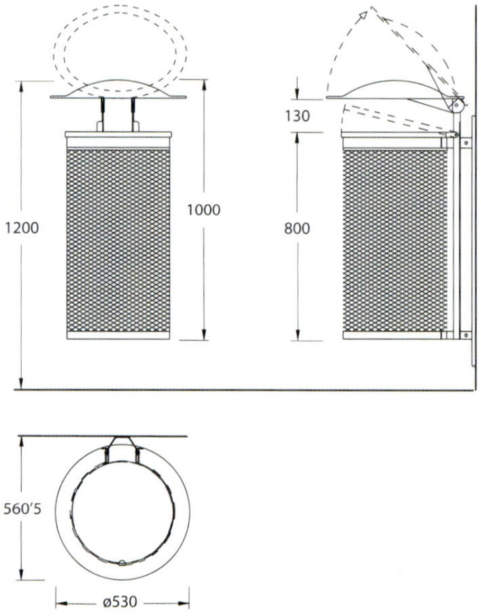

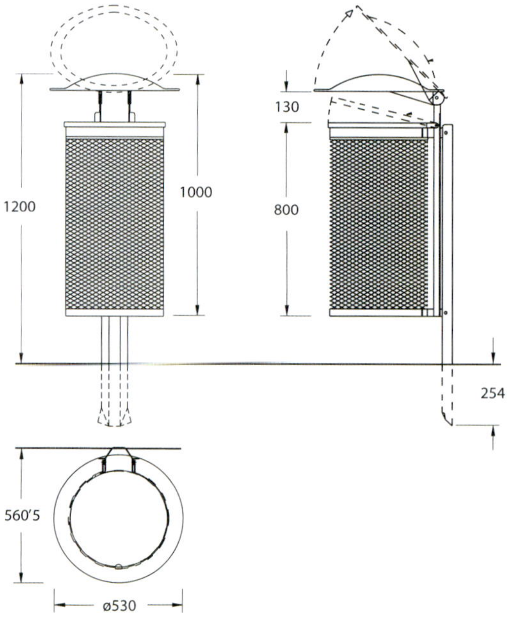

Saturno

Design: Brunetti Filipponi Associati
Production: ORA Centurelli

This square rubbish bin (single or double), which measures 300 x 300 mm (11,79 x 11,79 inches), is designed to be mounted on the Koh-JPost pole. It is made of perforated sheet metal on three sides, with square holes measuring 10 x 10 mm (0,4 x 0,4 inches) or rolled sheet metal 2 mm (0,783 inches) thick. The back is made of 2 mm (0,783 inches) thick sheet metal and has the attachments for hooking it onto the pole; there is also a plate with holes for the screws. The sheet metal lid is 3 mm (0,117 inches) thick. On request, cut-outs can be made through the lid using plasma or laser technology, in various shapes to make differentiated waste collection easier; the cut-outs can also be omitted. The available shapes are bottle, can, paper, battery, medicine; others can be requested. Hot-galvanizing according to UNI regulations and a choice of RAL paint coatings are available on request. The single waste bin dimensions are: Length, 780 mm (30,654 inches); Width, 290 mm (11,397 inches); Height, 900 mm (35,370 inches), with a capacity of 42 liters.

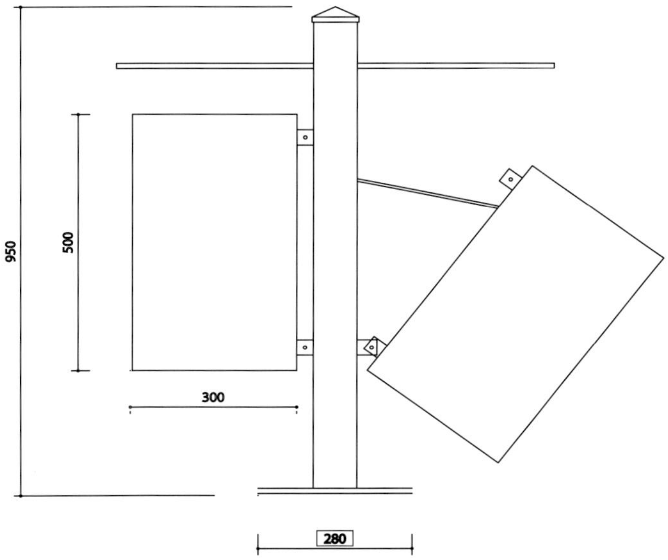

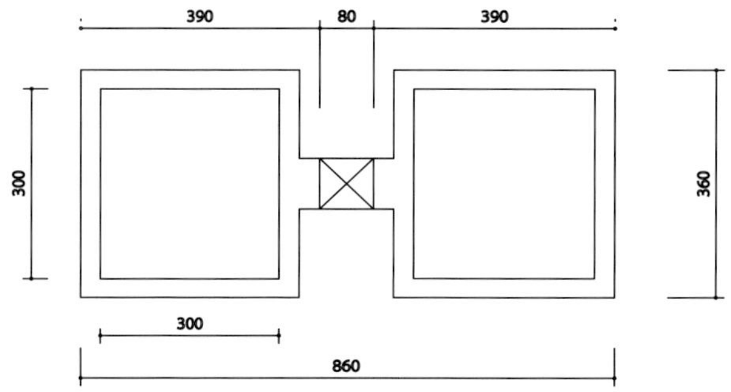

Valet

Design: David Karásek, Radek Hegmon
Production: mmcité

This slim and inconspicuous freestanding ashtray related to the SL bollards range is suitable for various localities. The article consists of a steel angle iron post that bears a lockable stainless steel box for cigarette ash or plastic bags for dog excrements. Its function is made identifiable by a cigarette symbol, engraved on the steel and enameled red to increase its visibility. Another model serves as a support of the plastic bags for dog excrements. The galvanized and powder coated steel body rises 1000 mm (39,3 inches) over the pavement. Two widths are available, to gain adaptability to the proportions of a given installation: L 60 mm (2,358 inches) and L 80 mm (3,144 inches). Its robust structure and easy manipulation are the major advantages of this modern element of street furniture. It has a baseplate designed to be fixed in the concrete under the pavement, guaranteeing the object's stability.

Argo

Design: Josep Suriñach
Production: Fundició Dúctil Benito

The Argo litter bin is triangular in plan, and consists of a reinforced steel sheet cube with laser-made holes. The cube element rests on a solid structure with a triangular base, which anchors it to the ground. The Argo litter bin looks exceedingly light, thanks to the texture of the cube and it's very fine legs. The structure is treated with the "Ferrus fdb" system, an iron protector process that guarantees a high resistance to rust. The main finish is Inde brown, but other options include oven-baked grey paint and stainless steel. A hinged grey cover is also available.

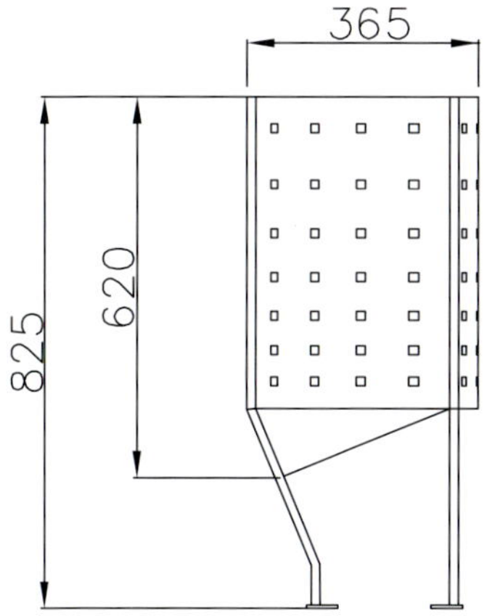

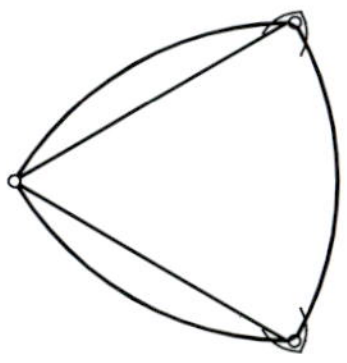

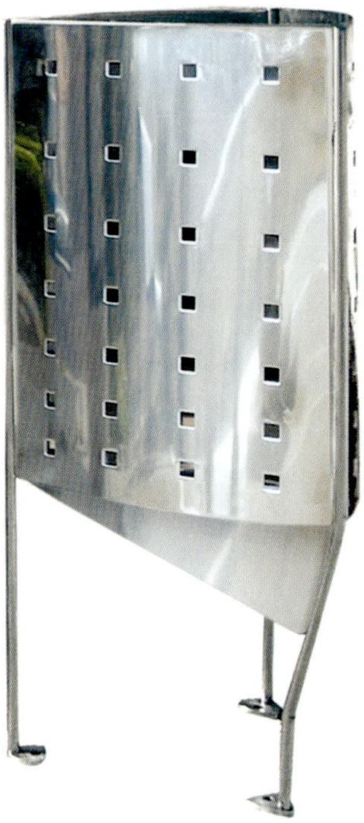

Canasto

Design: Diana Cabeza
Production: Estudio Cabeza

Especially in the version presented with a natural coloring, the basket-like form of this litter-bin transports us back to our origins and the thousand-year-old craft of ceramics and basket-weaving. Its tall and upright, almost proud outline, gives it a singular character, making the basket into an adequate design element for interior or outdoor furniture.

The item is made of pigmented polyethylene, roto-molded and with a sand-blasted surface finish. It is available in eight colors: red, tangerine, olive green, chlorophyll green, cobalt, sienna and purple. Designed to be merely rested on the ground without further anchoring devices, the Canasto litter-bin measures 440 mm (17.29 inches) in diameter and 850 mm (33.4 inches) in height.

Grace

Design: Sergio Fernández
Production: Tecam BCN

This stylish, elliptically shaped wastepaper basket consists of a bin in 2mm steel plate with the ring of the opening made in polished cast aluminum. It stands on two trapezoidal shaped legs. Its design allows it to have two dimensions in one, combining sturdiness and capacity with a slim, vertical line making it suitable for indoor and outdoor use.

It has a zinc coating fired in the oven to be oxyron grey or micro textured light grey.

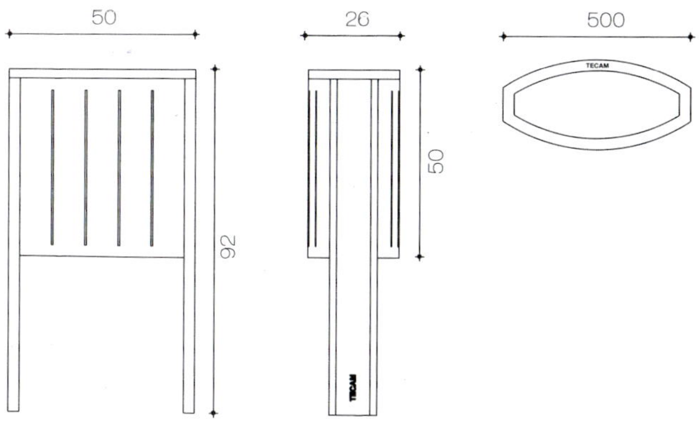

Fountains

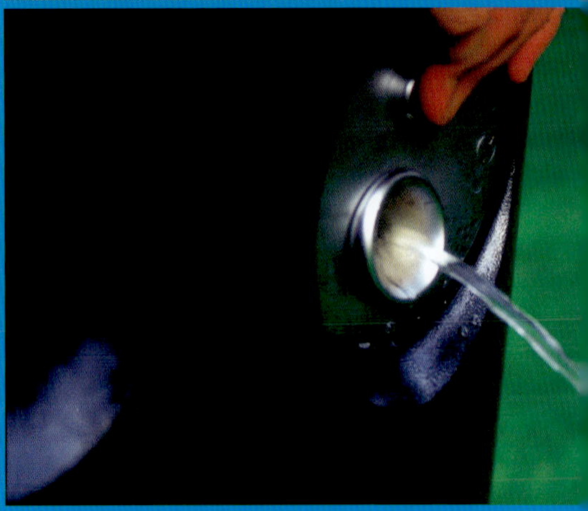

Chafariz

Design: Diana Cabeza Collaborators: L. Heine / M. Wolfson
Production: Estudio Cabeza

As a recreation of the traditional neighbourhood water spout, this dispenser for drinking water (or refreshing feet or head) solves the issue of providing water in public spaces. Ideal for refreshment after park games, or cycling, or during summer walks, the "chafariz" stands proud waiting for thirsty adults and children.
Both a totem and a user friendly play object, its steps and grab holes on the sides allow children to safely climb and drink.
The grate at the base is an embossed surface which, with little holes simulating water drops, contains water overflow. The lips of the spout keep the body dry.
Materials: Cast iron.
Finishing: Sand-blasted and color polyester thermosetting powder coated.
Size: Body: 17 x 40 x h=113.5 cm / Base: 60 x 150 x h=27 cm

Atlántida

Design: Enric Batlle-Joan Roig
Production: Santa & Cole

The Atlántida drinking fountain is good example of straightforwardly minimalistic urban design. It consists of a monolithic block of cast-iron, rust-protected and coated in black wrought-iron finish paint. The grid to collect the run-off water is made of the same material and rests within a frame made of corrosion-proof, hot-dip galvanized steel. The one-inch push-button spout is made of cast brass. The item is supplied in two separate parts: firstly, the block with its spout, and secondly, the grid and the water collection receptacle to be sunk into the ground. This fountain can be installed on its own or in a row. Various distributions are possible. The base is buried 10 cm into the ground and fixed into position with four anchoring bolts. The grid over the water collection receptacle at the base is the same width as the front of the fountain.

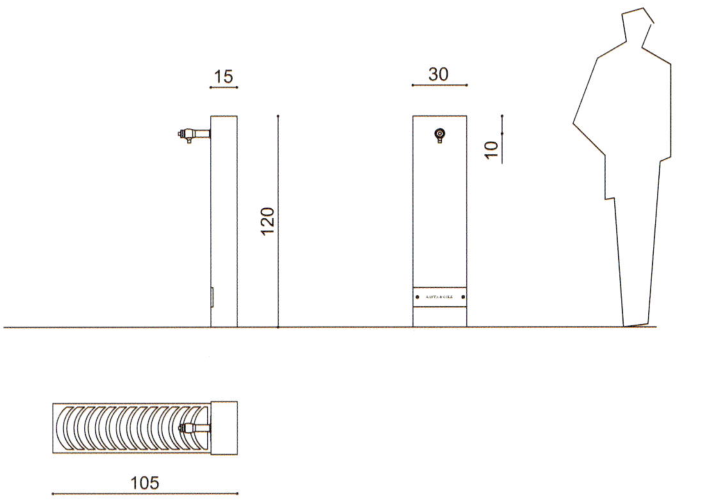

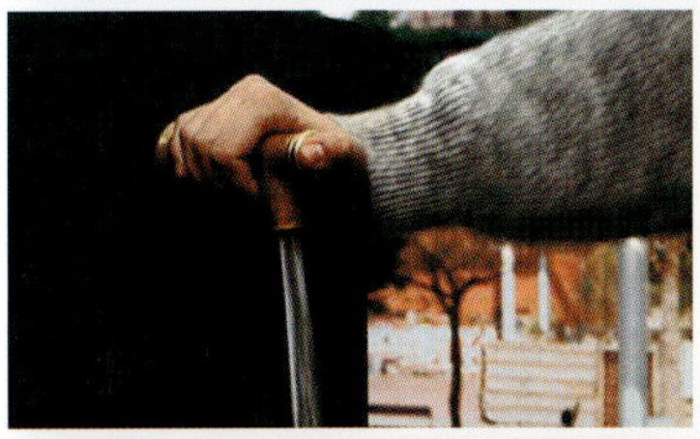

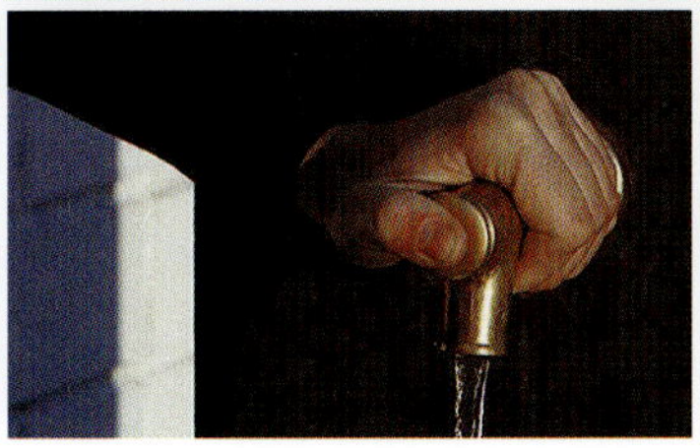

Fontfosa

Design: Pep Bonet
Production: DAE

Fontfosa is a notably sober-looking water fountain, made of cast iron with a black wrought-iron finish. The press-button is at the top and the stainless steel supply pipe is concealed under the fountain head, which has an inverted L-shaped cross section, avoiding anything that might disrupt the item's firm geometrical composition. The fountain drains directly into the base plate, where it is received by a grid installed flush with the pavement, thereby achieving a perfect integration with the surroundings it becomes part of. The article weighs 115 kg (253,46 lb), and is fixed in position by means of stainless steel anchoring bolts.

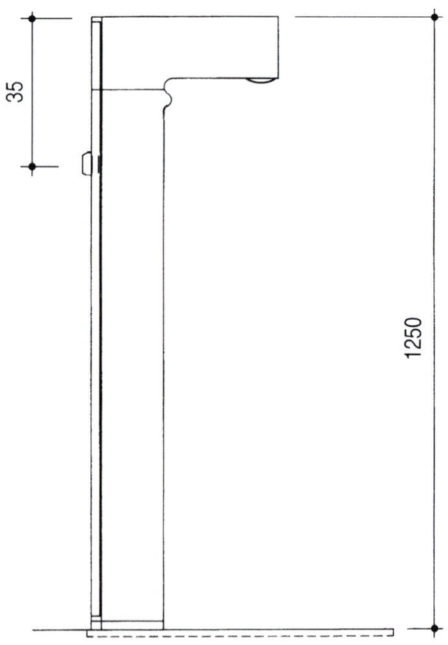

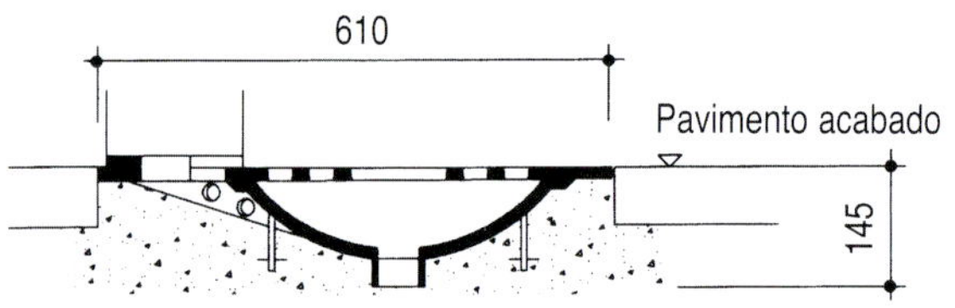

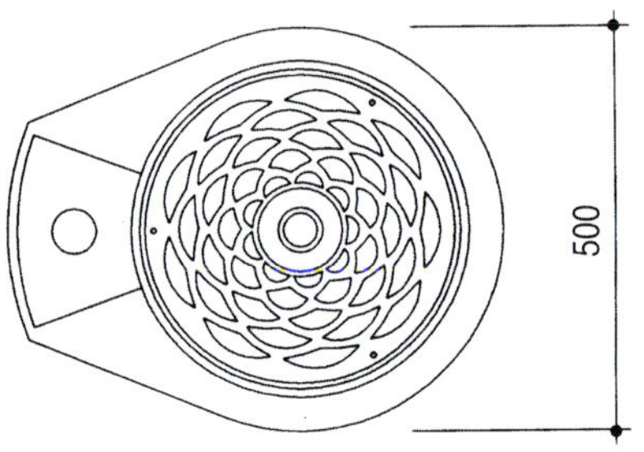

Agua

Design and Production: Geohide

There is little doubt that this drinking fountain is eye-catching because of its elegant sculptural shape, which in fact is a result of its purpose. "Agua" is actually a double water fountain: an upper one which comes out of the very top of the structure itself, and a lower one which is plate-shaped and easily reached by people in wheel chairs or small children. It is made entirely out of a highly resistant kind of stainless steel unaffected by corrosion. It measures 0.90 x 0.15 m (2907 x 5.89 inches) and is just over one meter (3.28 ft) high. The total weight is 60 kg (132.24 lb).

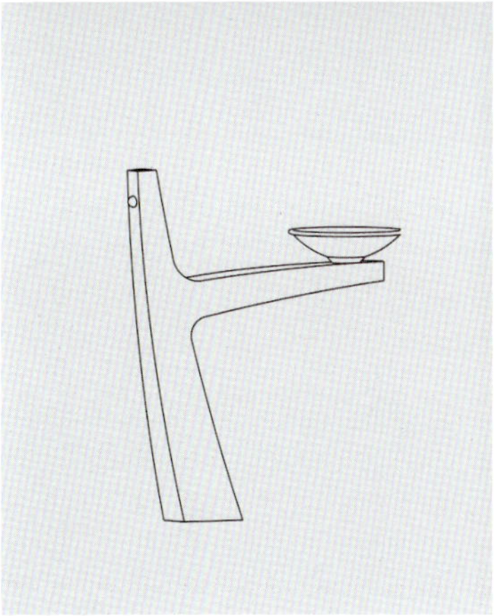

Radi

Design: Radi Designers

Proceeding as on previous occasions by associating ideas, Radi Designers won the award to the best realization in this competition. The intention was to renovate the shape of the public fountains in Paris, making access to the water more comfortable. After exploring a series of options, Radi decided that the original caryatid of the Wallace fountain had to play the leading part, enacting the gift of water instead of being a merely allegorical presence. Materializing the life-size form of a woman's body, the object consists of a revolving extrusion that joins two cut-outs, creating the volume. One of the arms on either side extends an open hand, from which the water flows; it is a natural looking object that makes the water easily accessible; although the figure is motionless, the directly comprehensible gesture achieved by Radi Designers is reminiscent of their successful Whippet Bench.

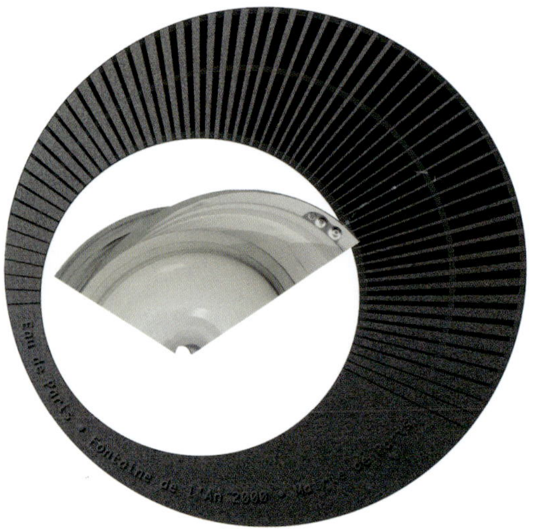

Naia

Design: Nuria Núñez
Production: DAE

This sturdy and robust drinking fountain is designed for installation in public spaces and outdoor areas. It consists of a slightly tapering inverted conical body made of cast iron, anodized and painted. Its upper part finishes in a slanted transversal section that reveals the fountain itself, with a push-button tap and a blue drainage basin that suggests the presence of water but in fact is a reflection of the sky with a silver grey finish.

The item's approximate weight is 96 kg (211.58 lb) and it is designed to be anchored to the pavement with stainless steel screws.

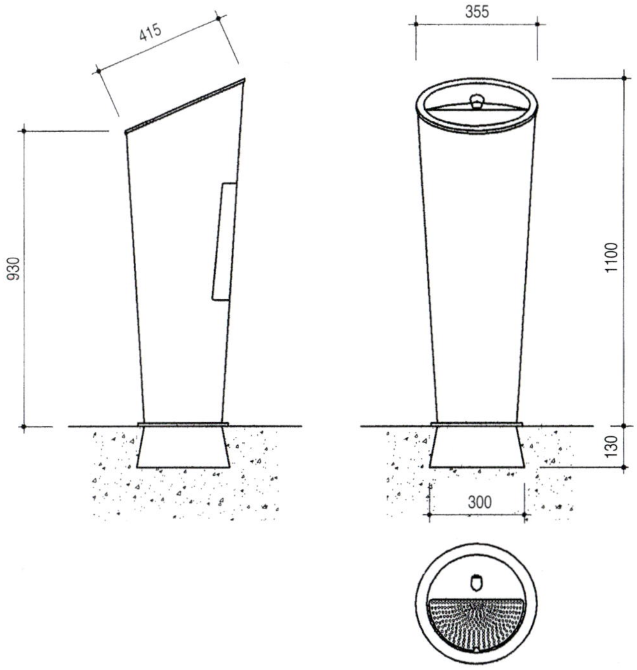

Lights

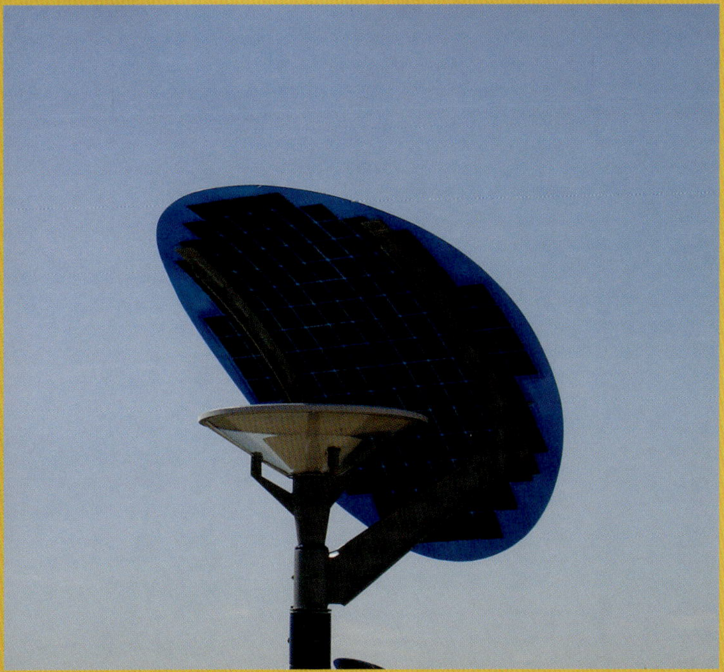

Bd Love lamp

Design: Ross Lovegrove
Production: Bd

This luminaire-bench is made of medium density polyethylene, rotomolded and pigmented in a range of different colors and with 8 stainless steel inserts at the base. The item can seat 3 people. The light diffuser screen is made of natural tone polyethylene of medium density with an additive against ultra violet rays. It is easy to disassemble for repair or changing the light source. There is a semi-gloss finished, cast aluminum (Al 2560) connection ring between the base and the diffuser screen. The piece contains the light source, a 230V 100W halogen lamp.
The luminaire-bench is available in the following colors: fluorescent red (only for indoor use), beige, white, blue, green, sandstone and millstone. It can also be supplied in special colors. The bases, each one of which measures 1.410 x 1.200 mm, can be stacked. Each unit has a height of 3000 mm (9.84') and weighs approximately 52 kg.

Sara

Design: Beth Galí
Production: Santa & Cole

The Sara street lamp arose from Beth Galí's project in the Irish city of Cork, between Saint Patrick's Street and Grand Parade. The designer wanted to create a unit that would reflect the asymmetrical nature of this crossroads, so she designed a street lamp with two different arms and two lighting systems; one is diffuse, the other is direct. The unit consists of two separate poles leaning at opposite angles and hinged together in the middle; this structure supports the two autonomous illumination systems, one for the street and the other for the pavement.

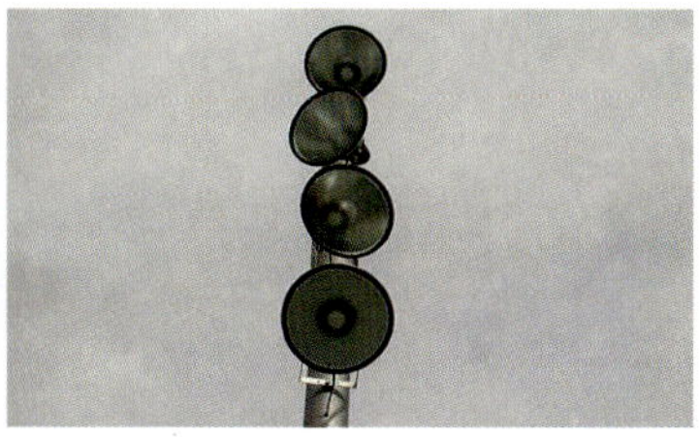

The tallest of the two poles tapers upward to the height of 10 meters (32.8 ft) and functions as the support for four PRX-327 discharge lamps projectors (maximum 250 W). The article is delivered without the wiring or the lamps. The other pole, which is 6 meters long (19,68 ft), supports two completely watertight HF-265 type luminaires with 58 W fluorescent lamps.

The item's five separate components are supplied ready to be assembled: the two poles, the axis that joins the two poles, the luminaires and the spotlight holders. The poles are fixed to the ground by means of anchoring bolts and concrete foundation blocks, cast in situ 24 cm (9.43 inches) beneath the pavement surface level. Construction of the foundation blocks must foresee an orifice to house the wiring ducts. The item's total weight is 382 kg (841.91 lb).

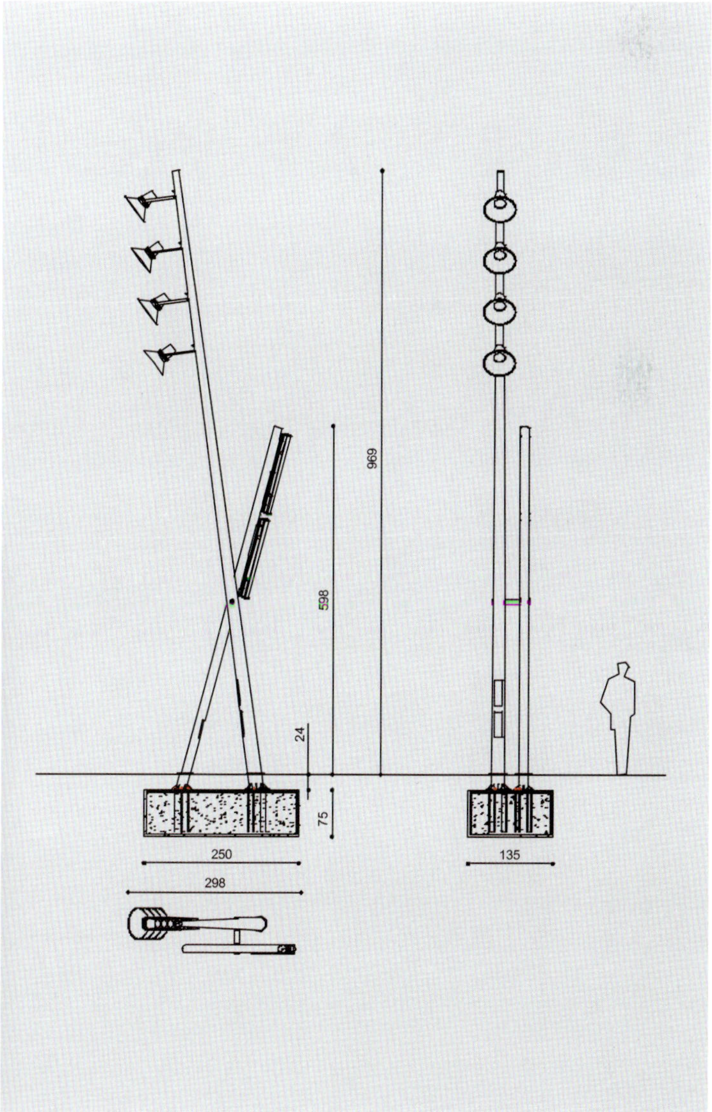

Totem

Design: Studio Itinerante Arquitectura
Production: Siarq

The Totem has a double role as both a streetlight and a photovoltaic plant for generating energy. Its 16 m (52.48 ft) high vertical structure is made of laminated wood. Incorporated into the very top of the structure are two 250 W floodlights which light the surrounding area sufficiently but at the same time guard against light pollution. The plant can generate up to 3,400 kWh of energy which is transferred to the public power supply network, while the energy needed for the floodlights, less than half of what it generates, comes directly from the conventional electric system. In addition to these two functions this structure also creates a recreational area at ground level, which makes it particularly appealing for public spaces. The design of the structure has taken into account more than just aesthetic criteria; the technical and mechanical aspects necessary for generating energy, providing adequate lighting and easy maintenance were given equal importance.

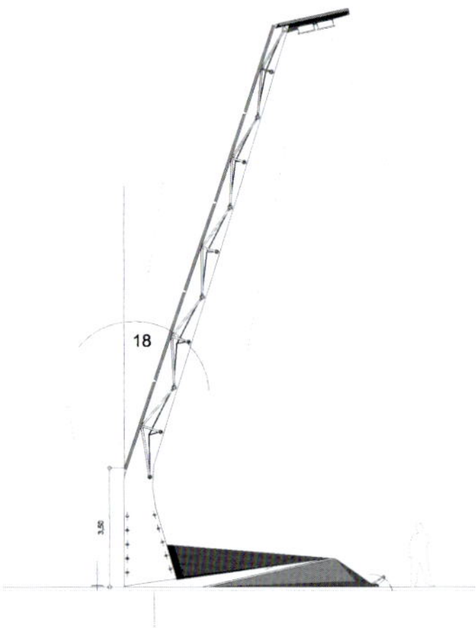

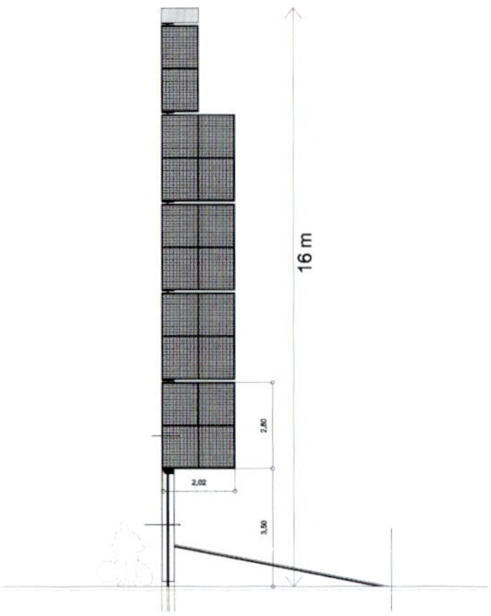

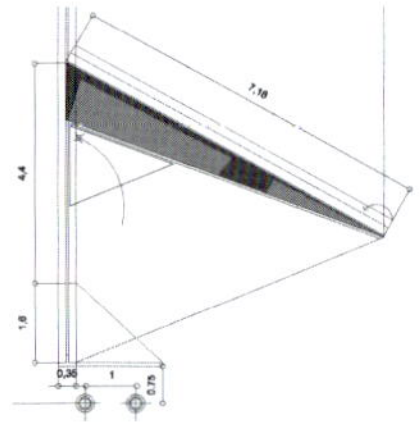

Ballerina

Design and Production: Geohide

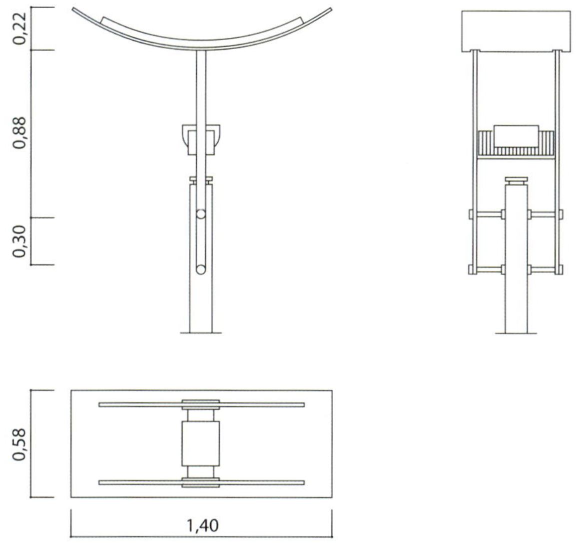

Ballerina is a symmetrical street lighting fixture designed for pedestrian areas. It consists of two main components, the support post and the luminaire. The support post consists of a hollow steel cylinder, 130 mm in diameter, rising 3.30 meters (10.82 ft) above the ground, galvanized and painted. Other finishes can be supplied on demand.

The luminaire consists of the system that attaches it to the post, the lamp holder, the light source and the reflector. The light source is a watertight projector with an HGI – TS 75W or 150W halogen lamp; the other accessories together measure 1.40 x 0.58 m (55.02 x 22.8 inches), and weighs approximately 55 kg. (121 lb)

The lamp sheds a warm indirect light which is evenly distributed around the post, avoiding the discomfort and harsh visual effect of directly seeing the light source. It is possible to adapt the luminaire onto new or existing poles of variable diameters (max. 0.34 m / 13.36 inches). The fixture has a self-stabilized fastening by means of two transoms. As it is entirely made of stainless steel, it is highly resistant and unalterable. The system can be easily and swiftly assembled. The surface finish is sandblasted (other finishes are available upon request).

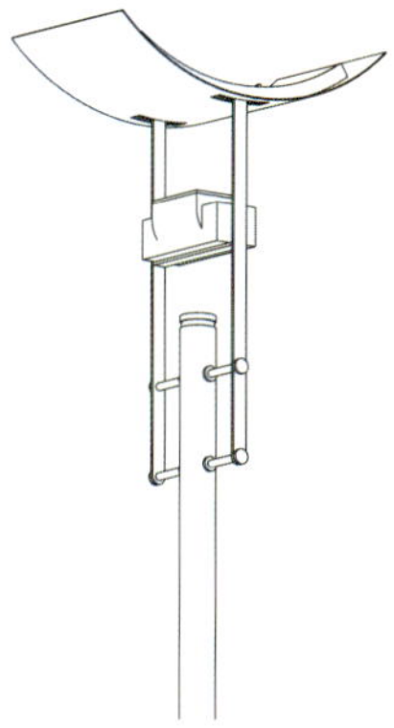

Mawson Lakes Solar Light

Design and Production: Street and Park Furniture

A major Australian developer, keen to demonstrate his commitment to the sustainable use of resources such as water and electricity, commissioned a design which would do just that in the field of energy. A team from the company Street and Park Furniture were chosen for the job: the resulting solar light is now functioning in the Mawson Lakes area. The striking aspect of this solar-energy light is its unusual curved photovoltaic panel, which was also designed by the same company. As most solar panels are not noted for their interesting design, this curved panel has brought a kind of dynamism to the light while softening the visual impact of the light source. In order to produce a curved solar panel the manufacturers had to perform a lot of trials before finding the best solution. In addition these lights had to be able to light the path so combining design and function was all-important. The mechanism consists of a single curved solar panel of laminated fiberglass, with metallic components of mild steel and aluminum. The solar panel is like a large oval-shaped visor on what seems to be a conventional lamppost. Apart from capturing the sun's energy during the day it acts as a luminous screen at night when the lamp is lit.

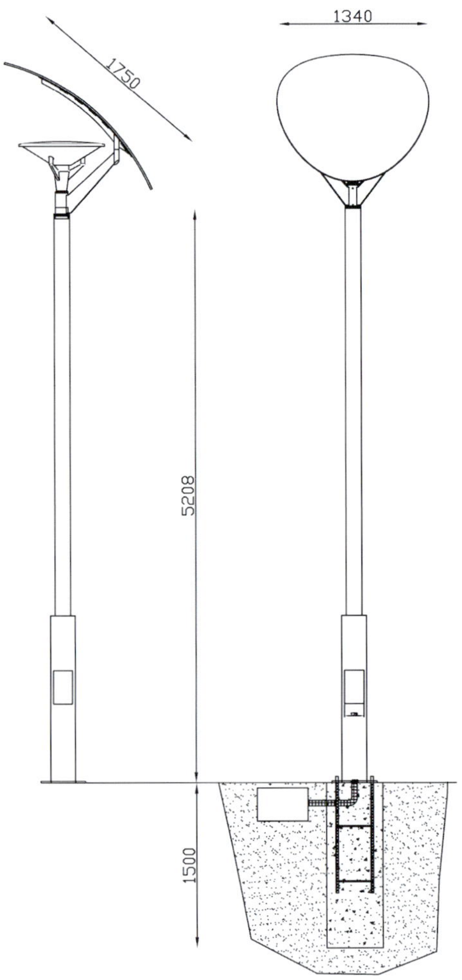

Triangel

Design and Production: **Philips**

Triangel combines a strong, easily remembered design with a robust and durable construction. Its characteristic lit triangle at the top creates an optical guidance and secondary lighting. It is designed for use in residential areas, shopping areas, car parks, footpaths/pedestrian areas and other urban spaces where its high efficiency reflectors will provide economic lighting. Tempered safety glass makes Triangel vandal-resistant.

The housing is made of robust, die-cast aluminum, painted in black or grey (RAL 7021). The cover is made of tempered safety glass - frosted (GF) or clear (GC) - mounted in an aluminum frame, painted in the color of the housing. The article weighs approximately 12 kg (26,5 lb). It is suitable for a wide variety of lamp types. Mounting brackets are available to permit single, double or quadruple post top mounting.

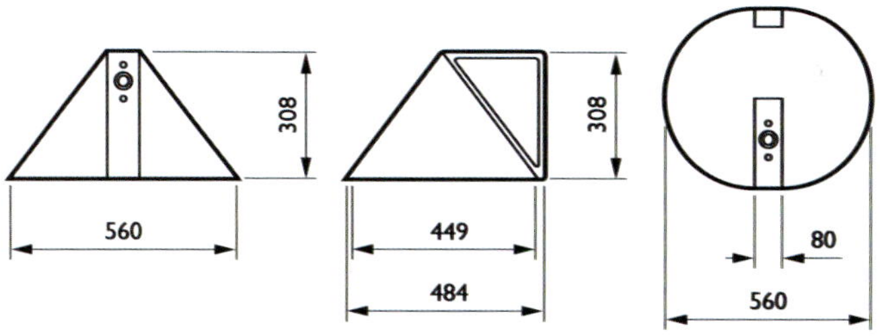

Vrellen

Design: UTGM & DA2
Production: Ghisamestieri

The Vrellen lighting bracket combines function and elegance by using an innovative material for outdoor lighting: the arm connecting the luminaire to the pole is made of structural glass, supported by an almost imperceptible aluminum section. Vrellen is a product range comprising poles of various heights, luminaires in two different sizes, and wall brackets, for different areas of a city to be illuminated by a coherently designed range of articles.
The luminaire is of pressure die-cast aluminum in conformity with CEI regulations. The protection degree is IP 66; made of extra-pure anodized aluminum with a flat, tempered glass lens, the reflector casts a non-symmetrical, mainly transversal light. It has an extractable bayonet plastic shutter, for lamp replacements; heat-resistant rubber gaskets protect the optical compartment. No light is cast upward, following the strictest regulations regarding luminus contamination. The item is 263 mm (10.33 inches) high, Ø600 mm (23.58 inches) wide, and weighs 15 kg (6,80 lb plus wiring).

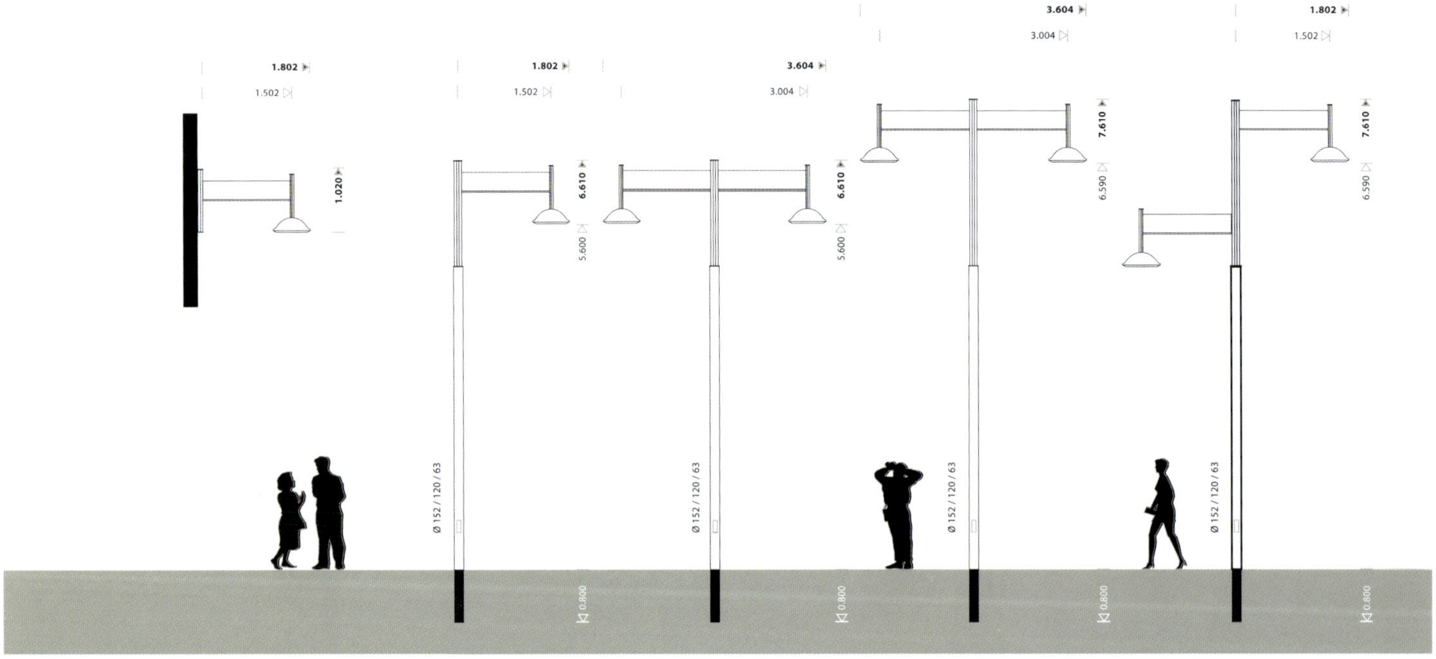

Tournesol

Design: Philippe Starck
Production: JC Decaux

The Tournesol (Sunflower) streetlight has the unmistakable stamp of a Philippe Starck design. Its originality lies in the lamp's movement: during the day it is in a vertical position but at night it bends over to light the way for pedestrians in the street. It is therefore an enigmatic urban sculpture by day and at night reveals its main function thanks to the rotating lamp head. The shape and texture of the post have a distinctly biological feel which together with the fact it moves, reinforces this idea of being almost "alive" which makes it even more attractive.

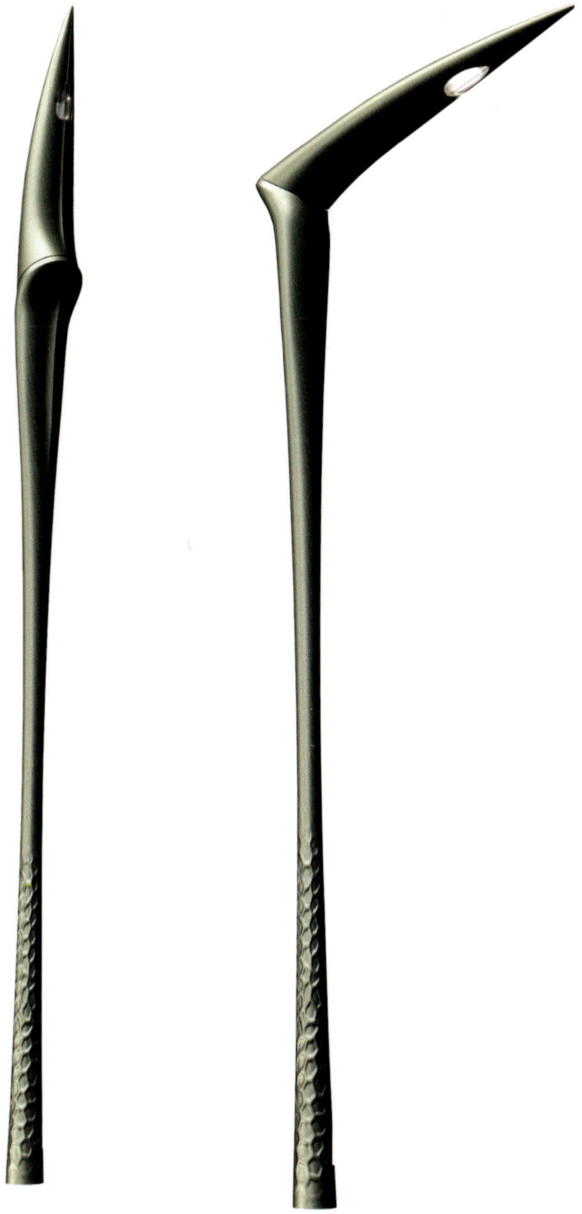

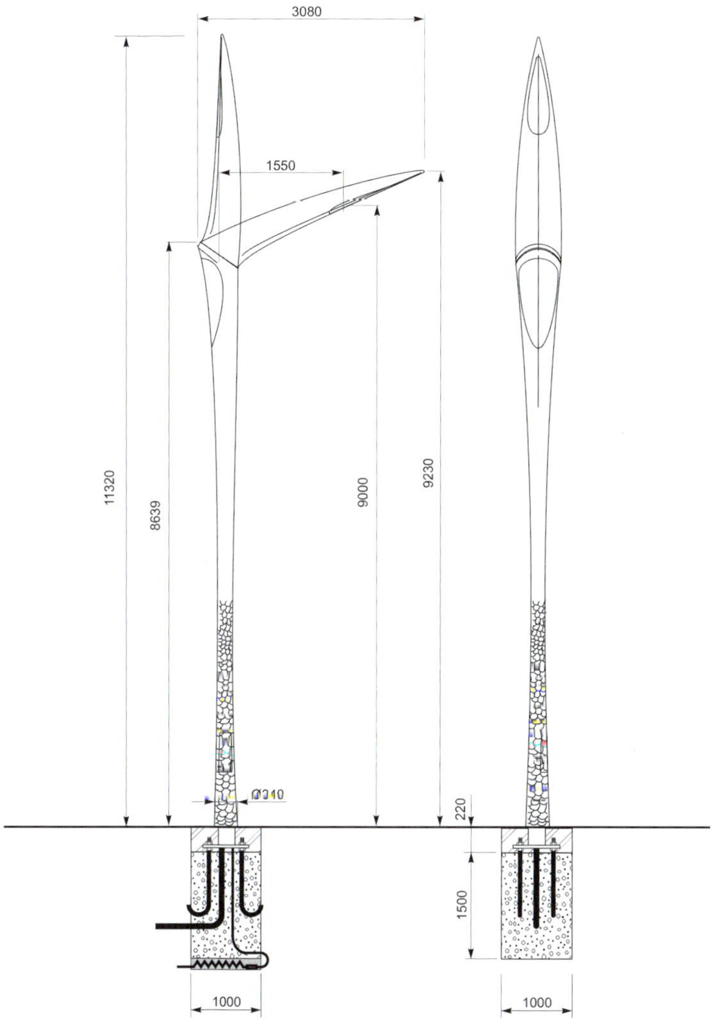

Faro

Design: Lichtlabor Bartenbach / Klaus Begasse
Production: Hess Form + Licht

The innovative technical concept of the Faro collection is made clearly evident by the characteristics of its design that is based on a secondary, faceted, square reflector, which is made of a special plastic that also reflects the sunlight to great effect during the hours of daylight. The body of the luminaire itself, with a primary source of light and reflection, displays a formal unity with the lamp post, adopting a separate, conical configuration by means of a simple line of shadow. This creates a counterpoint to the secondary reflector located further up, thereby transmitting an overall effect of simplicity that is easy to integrate harmoniously into any environment. The illumination generated in this way is non-blinding, symmetrical and indirect. To achieve a desirable adaptation to different lighting requirements, the posts are supplied in a variety of lengths, with correspondingly adapted secondary reflectors.

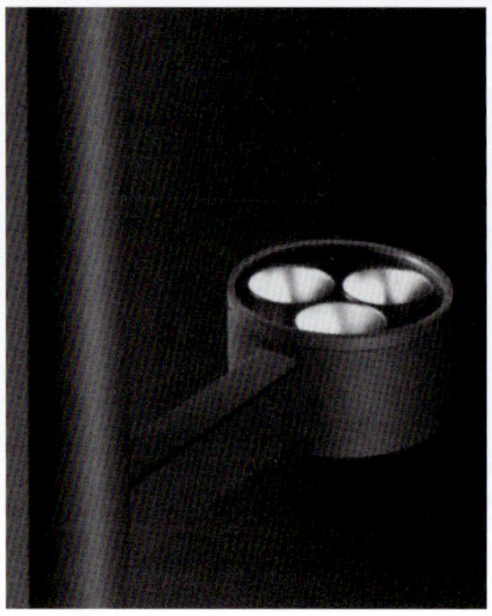

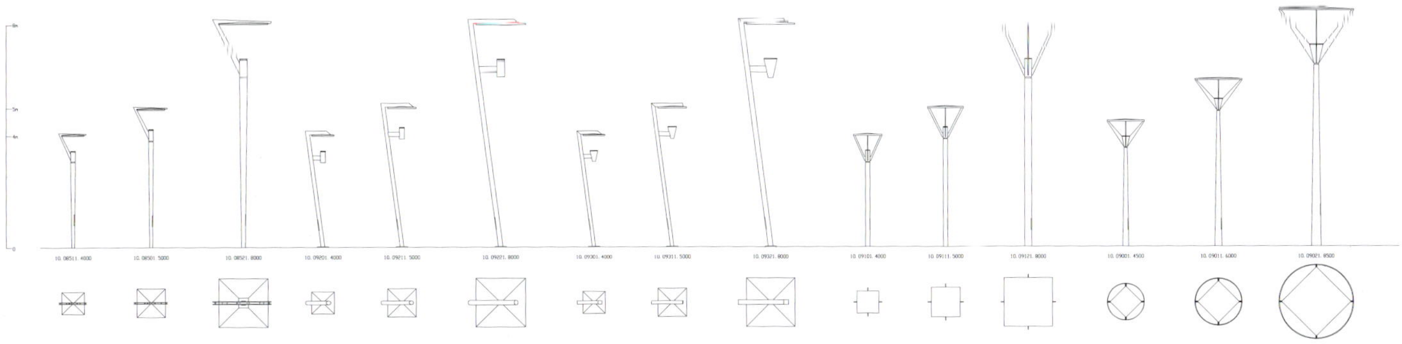

LLum-i

Design: Albert Viaplana / Helio Piñón
Production: Escofet

Llum-i is a sculpture by day and an atmospheric lamp by night. With its strong geometric lines this piece plays with light and shade and the concrete shapes. It is an ideal lamp for pedestrian areas, with a real sense of human scale, good for marking out routes or alternatively on a larger scale, when several units are grouped together, they turn into a landmark. Made out of reinforced concrete and stainless steel the finish is a granite grey color, stripped and waterproofed. Each piece is anchored down with screws and weighs 340 kg (749 lb).

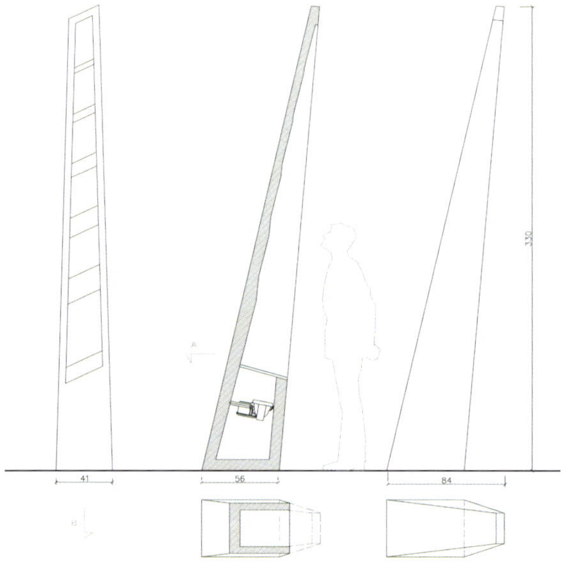

Kanya

Design: Olga Tarrassó, Jordi Henrich, Jaume Artigues, Miquel Roig
Production: Escofet

The Kanya series of lampposts is intended for lighting large areas, particularly suitable for urban environments and public spaces. They consist of tapered columns in Cor-Ten steel, stainless steel or galvanized steel and stand at an angle of 85º. The heights vary (10, 12 or 15m / 32.20, 39.36 or 49.2 ft). When several are grouped together but facing different ways, attractive lighting effects can be achieved, with endless possibilities thanks to the flexibility of how the pole is positioned and the angle the lights are set at. The column holds circular parabolic floodlights, the number of which varies according to the selected height.

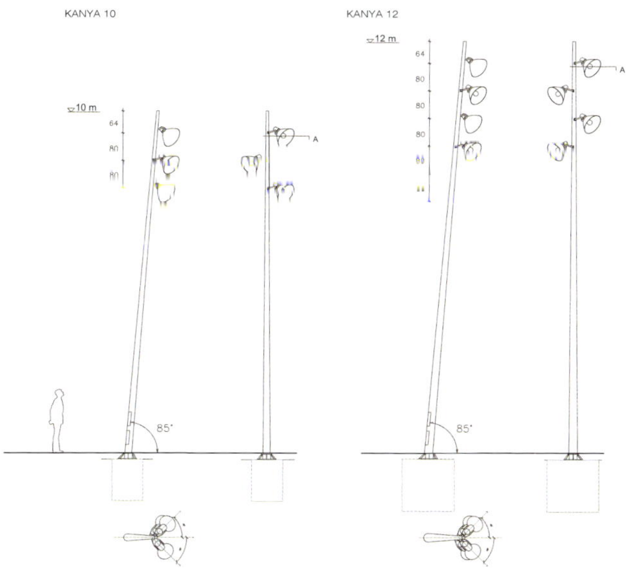

Arona

Design: Enrico Marforio
Production: Ghisamestieri

This collection is characterized by a special care for the optimisation of light effects through wise handling of their chromatic aspects. In fact the sinuous lines of its elements are put in evidence and emphasized by the harmonic use of color, which becomes a protagonist in urban areas.

The Arona Collection consists of several light-reflecting elements (post-top luminaire or light pole with fibreglass diffuser) customizable in their finish and chromatic components. This assures countless composition possibilities. The lighting elements are part of a complete collection consisting of bollards, park benches and refuse containers suitable to offer flexible and functional solutions for the decoration of city areas.

The luminaire mounted on the lamp-post Arona for pedestrian areas, public parks and gardens is in conformity with CEI regulations. It is made of a cylinder-shaped steel body consisting of a tube, Ø150 mm (5.89 inches) in diameter, and various shaped plates where the optical group is inserted; aluminium plate diffuser, white painted on underside, in order to reflect the light from the optical compartment; three steel arms screwed to the cylindrical body, to support the aluminium diffuser.

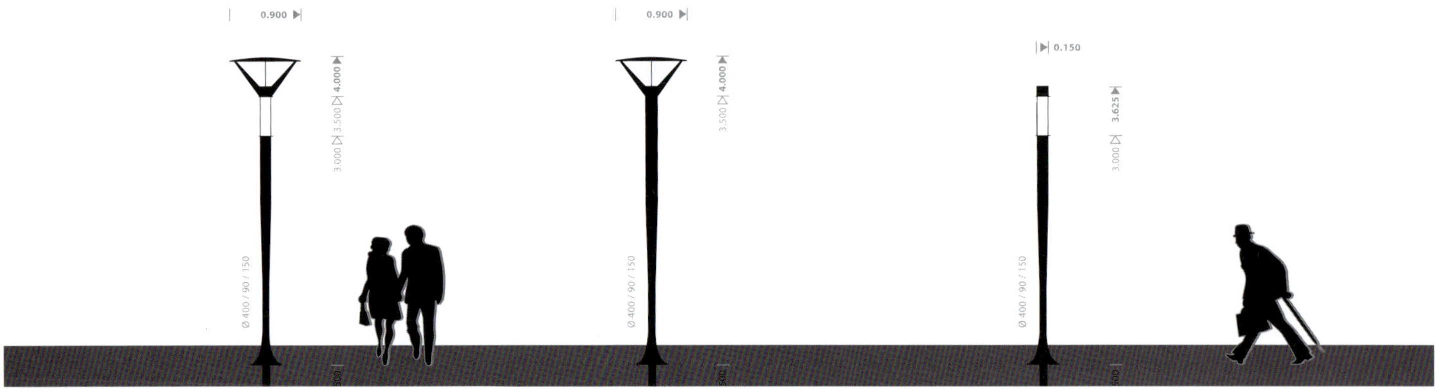

Rondò

Design: Piero Ravaioli
Production: Ghisamestieri

The suppression of road crossings, gradually transformed into stream roundabouts, has induced Ghisamestieri to design the Rondò system as the answer to the need to find a pleasant way to illuminate and decorate these new urban areas that are now integral parts of any urban landscape. Its harmonic light shape and the chromatic central obelisk consent the creation of different setting solutions, in accordance with the background where it is placed.
The Rondò system is proposed as a completely flexible decorative solution, thanks to three different types of obelisk with different windows of various types, and three curved tapered columns of different heights.

Dinosaurio

Design: Studio Itinerante Arquitectura
Production: Siarq

Beyond the function of illuminating the public space in which it is located, this street lamp incorporates the task of being a solar energy power plant producing photovoltaic energy. With a maximum height of 13 meters (42.64 ft), it carries two projectors of 250W and 400W, besides its 18 solar panels with a photovoltaic surface of 25 sqm (269 sqft). The system is capable of generating up to 3.800 kWh per year. All the energy captured this way is fed directly into the power supply system; likewise, the energy consumed by the light projectors –about half of the amount that the system generates- is acquired from the regular supply line. The electrical bill amounts to the difference between the energy provided and the energy consumed. The item itself is an innovative piece of public sculpture in which the solar panels are an added part of the design. Their inclination and the sculpture's curves instill a dynamic sensation to the composition; likewise, the colorful combination of materials, Corten steel and the techno-bluish panels create an exciting vibration between the sculpture and the environment.

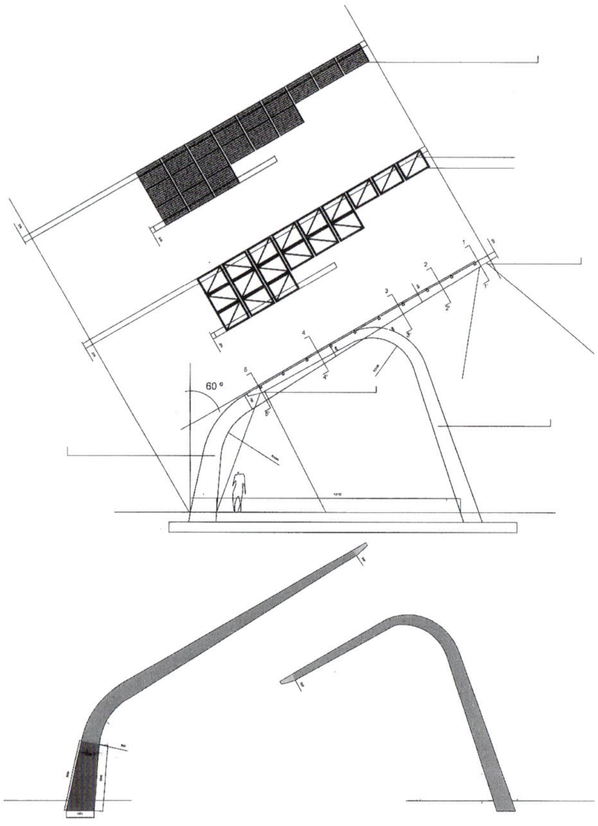

Kipp Post

Design: Alfred Homann
Production: Louis Poulsen

Kipp Post emits symmetrical downlight. The conical angle of the inner diffuser together with the slightly curved design of the top shade ensures a wide and uniform distribution of the light. The internal diffuser furthermore provides optimal glare-free lighting. Optional finishes are textured and aluminium colored or powder coated grey.

The diffuser is made of high-pressure molded opalescent-white acrylic resin or white spun aluminium. The top shade is black or white pigmented, injection molded ASA. The enclosure is made of injection moulded clear polycarbonate. The frame is die cast aluminum.

The various pole options measure (at top): Ø 60mm; Ø 76mm; the QL version Ø 115mm.

Installation cable: 4m, 2x1mm^2 or 4m, 3x1mm^2. Terminal block: 1x2x2.5mm^2 or 1x3x2.5mm^2.

Glowing Places

Design and Production: **Philips**

Glowing Places is a concept from an investigation into innovative ways for people to interact with light in public spaces. The plastic seating, embedded with LED (light-emitting diode) strips and sensors, measure the presence of people over time. Both the number of people sitting and the length of time they stay create a 'social interactive pattern' that is translated by patented software into lighting effects in the furniture. Many people sitting for brief periods of time result in lighting activity expressing a busy period, whereas one or two people sitting for a longer period trigger mellow lighting.

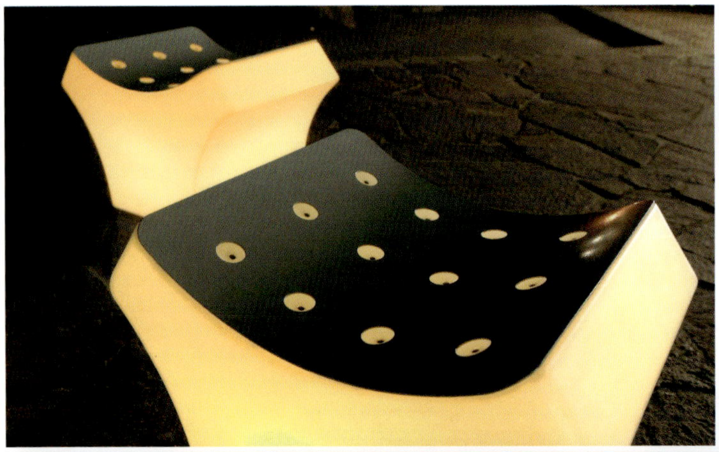

Ruta del Quijote

Design: Guillermo Sánchez Gil
Production: Tecnología y Diseño Cabanes

Stamped with the mark XQ, "IV Centenario Ruta del Quijote", the creation of this traffic beacon arises from an initially simple flat rectangle that unfolds vertically. It is almost entirely made of 3 mm thick Corten steel plate; the light diffuser is made of stainless steel sheet; the base is a 5 mm thick rectangle of steel plate, anchored to the ground or the pavement. The electrical equipment consists of an IP-67 luminaire with an energy saving 18 W lamp. Access to the electrical system is through an opening at the top of the object, closed by a personalized lid. The result of directing the light from the source towards the pavement is an agreeable indirect illumination that makes everything seem to glow, enhancing the environment of the immediate surroundings.

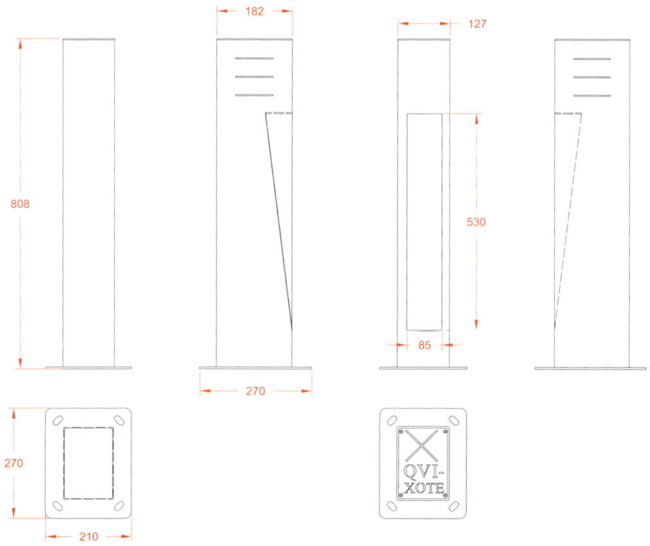

Yumi

Design: DA2
Production: Ghisamestieri

The wish to tidy up and make room for one piece in the place of the great deal of elements filling our pavements originated the lighting system Yumi. This name echoes oriental essentiality and the shape a Japanese Samurai's long ancient bow called Yumi. This new system integrates street lighting and decoration.
Three long curved tubes support the luminaire starting from the base where an integrated planter, or a litter bin on request, is incorporated. The light flux emitted by the Yumi system in its upper hemisphere is null, in conformity with the strictest regulations concerning luminus contamination.
The Yumi system consists of of three circular section steel tubes, 4mm thick, 60mm in diameter. One of the three poles is provided with a screw M10 (earthing), and with a slot where the electric wiring goes in to feed the luminaire.
The lower body has the purpose of holding the three tubes and, at the same time, it can house a planter (standard version) or a litter bin. Furthermore, a flange is welded to the lower portion of the body for ground fastening. Yumi is supplied with self-supporting base (1700 x 1700 mm / 5.57 x 5.57 inches).

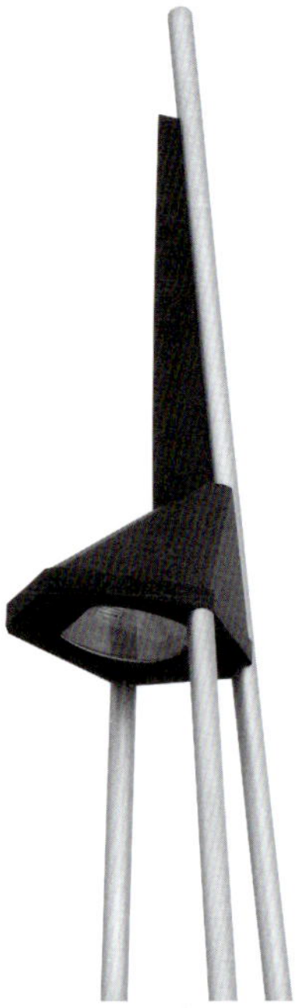

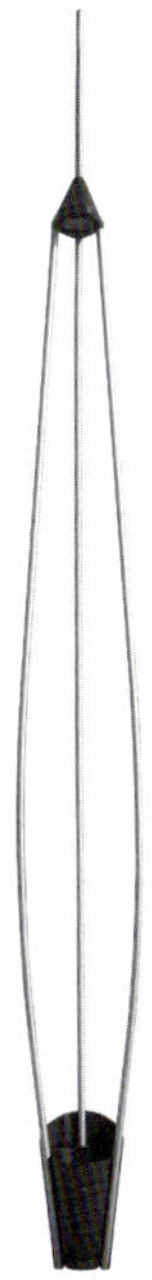

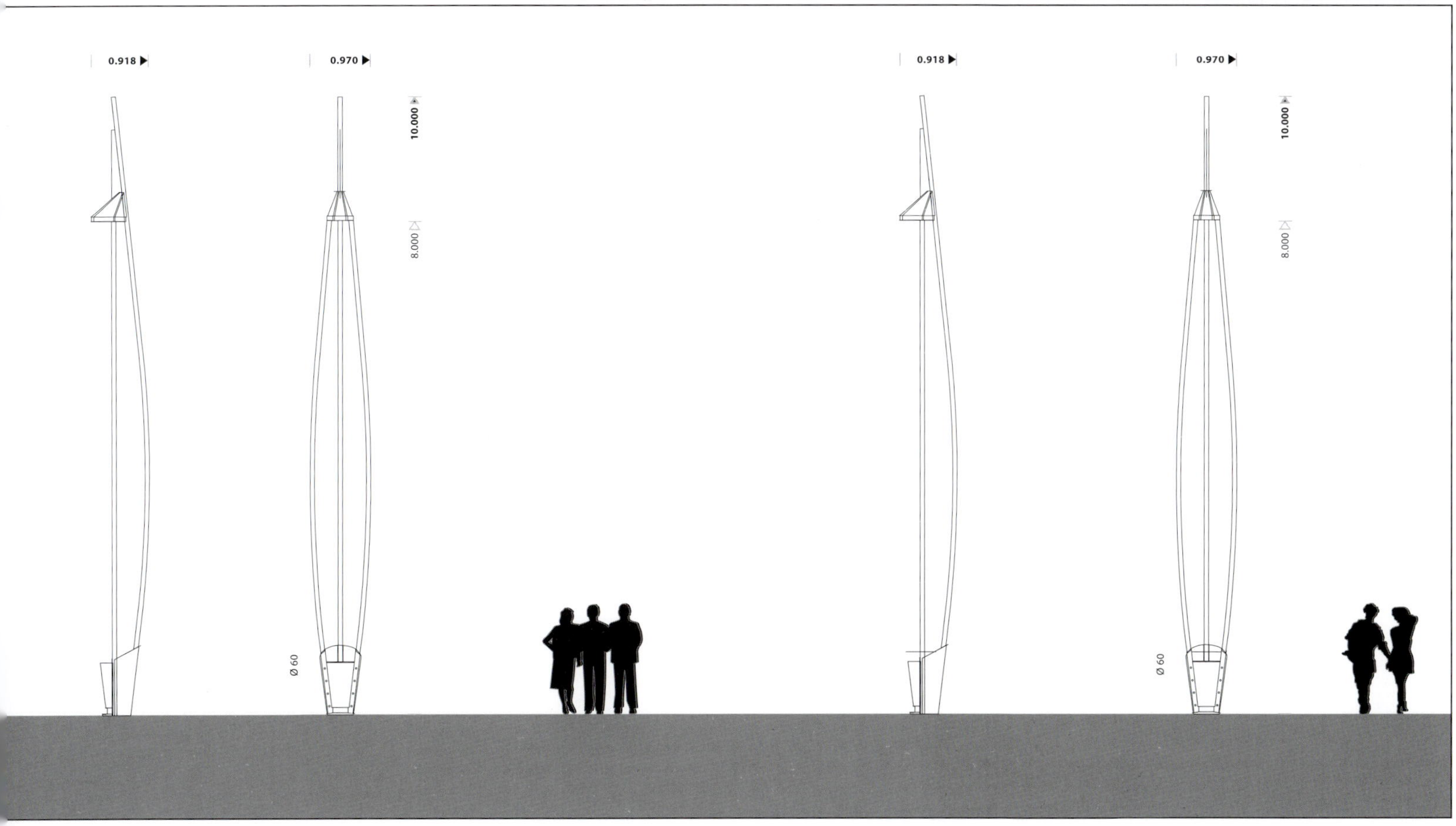
0.918
0.970
10.000
8.000
Ø 60
0.918
0.970
10.000
8.000
Ø 60

Rama

Design: Gonzalo Milà
Production: Santa & Cole

Simple, innovative and versatile, Rama (in Spanish: branch) consists of a cylindrical lamp-post designed to carry one or more lamps, fitted to the post, with clamps. The branches of this "light tree" fulfill a threefold objective: to avoid luminous contamination light is cast downwards to the pavement, the consumtion of electrical power is reduced to a minimum and the system opens the possibility of installing a variable number of luminaires at different heights and positions. The various types of illumination it provides, make the item suitable for any urban area.

The posts are 129 mm(5.07 inches) in diameter and are available in different heights: 4,70m (15.41 ft), 6m (19.68 ft) and 8m (26.24 ft). The material used is hot-galavanized steel or stainless steel AISI 304* with a polished finish texture. The luminaire and its clamp or made of injected grey polyamide, with an aluminum reflector and a tempered glass diffusor lens. This fixture is designed for compact fluorescent lamps of 57 to 70 W or high pressure discharge sodium vapor lamps or metal halide lamps.

Anchoring bolts fix the foot of the lamp post to a concrete foundation cube buried under the pavement.

Each single or double luminaire weighs: (single) 8kg | (double) 13,5 kg. The post weighs 88 kg (193.95 lb)

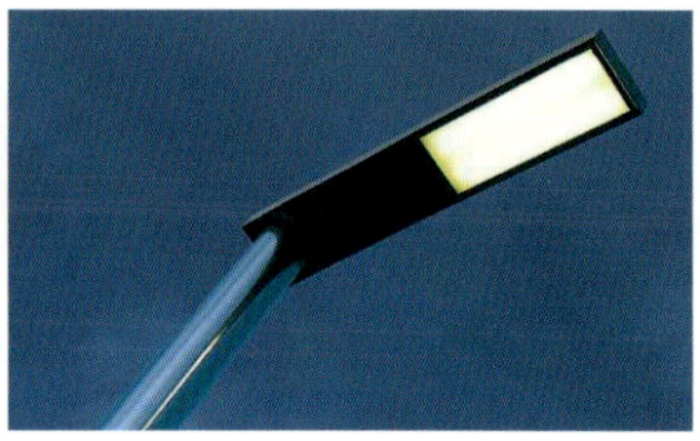

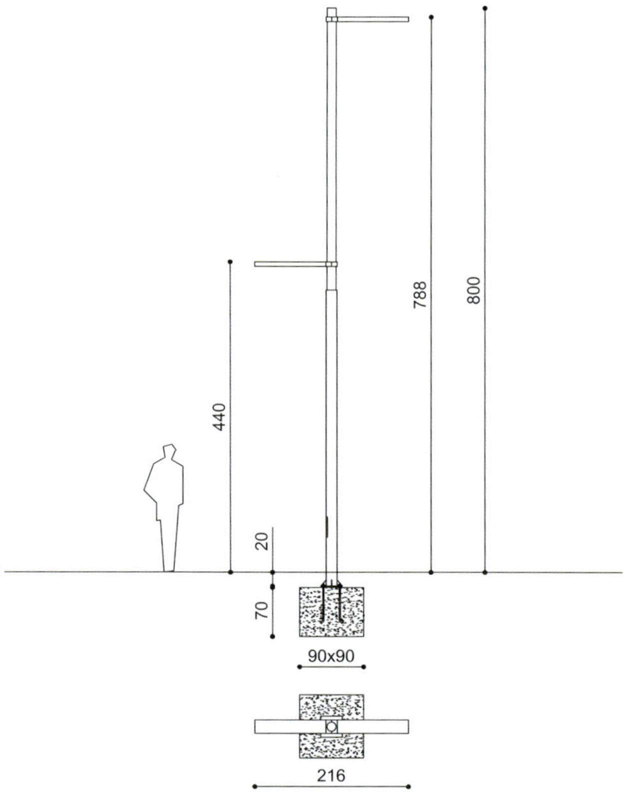

AJC

Design and Production: **Microarquitectura**

This streetlamp with projected lighting is built like a telescope with the upper part emerging from a square casing.
The AJC light embodies the contemporary style of floodlight often seen today, but is a far cry from the cold, technical image which has a tendency to be too simplistic.
Its elegant appearance comes partly from the materials used – the effective combination of painted iron with stainless steel, and partly because of the lamp's sleek, geometric lines.
The range of models offers versatility with two heights as well as the option of hanging varied combinations of lights at different heights. This makes it possible to illuminate different kinds of areas, whether they be roads, pedestrian zones, town squares or open spaces.

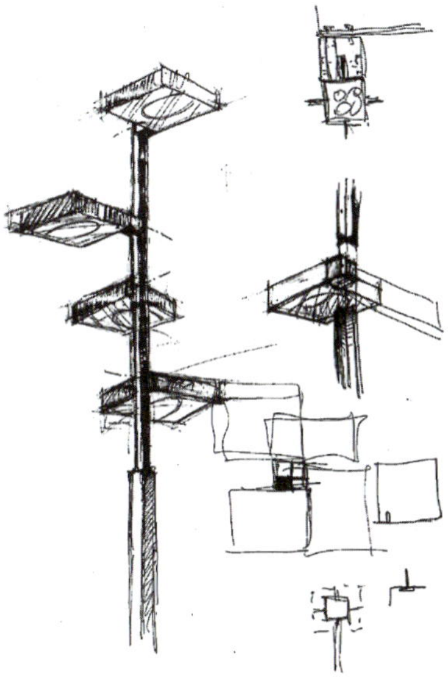

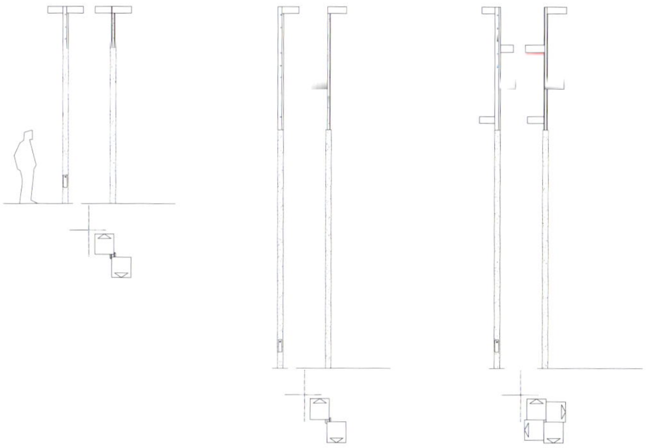

Poniente

Design: Silvia López
Production: Macaedis

The design of Poniente has been carried out with the intention of building a light fixture to provide indirect lighting that will not only conceal the light source, but also enhance the natural qualities of the material it is made of. The result is a singularly sculptural piece of urban furniture that illuminates itself and establishes a visual landmark within the area in which it has been installed. It is available in a wide variety of colors, according to the type of natural stone out of which it has been made: Alhambra yellow marble, Eneus marble, white Macael marble, Capri limestone, Iberian cream, black Marquina marble, golden Travertine or green Macael. The item measures 160 x 240 x 650 mm (6.28 x 9.43 x 25.54 inches) and its weight is 28 Kg (61.71 lb). It is designed to be anchored to the ground by means of corrugated steel rods fixed into the pavement.

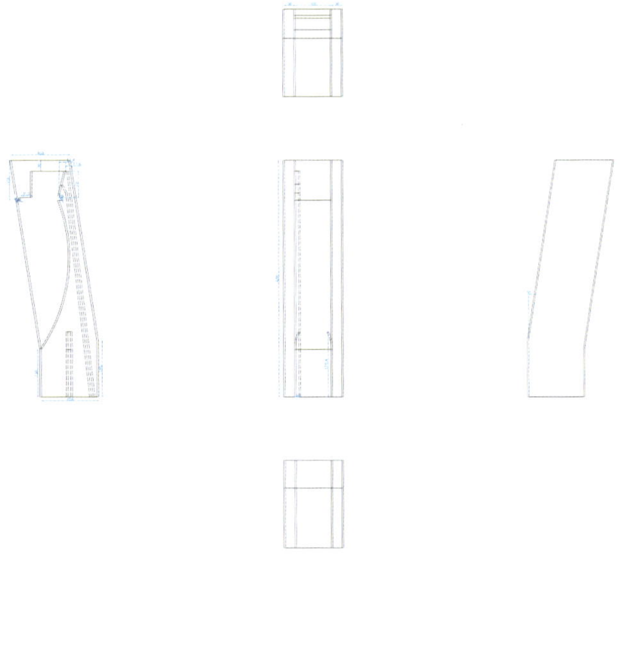

Upupa

Design and Production: **Geohide**

This indirect lighting system is designed to shed ambient light onto a limited perimetral area, namely onto the banners or flags hanging from the upper part of the poles, giving them a preponderant visual and symbolic role after dark, while providing a subtle light over the area around the flagpole. Installed in groups, a dynamic installation can be choreographed. The luminaire can be adapted to the tops of existing flagpoles or the flagpole accessory can be used.

The pole accessory is a conical cylinder, tapering upward from Ø 0.15m at the base, to Ø 0.07 m at the top, 9 meters (29.52 ft) above the ground.

The pole is made of brushed aluminum (other finishes are available on demand).

The light source is an HQI 35 W halogen lamp.

The luminaire fixture itself (fastener to pole+lamp holder+hat) measures 0.30 m (11.79 inches) in diameter, 0.45 m (17.68 inches) in height, and weighs approximately 1 kg (2.2 lb). It is made of aluminum and has three fins at 120 degree intervals, that project upward to support the hat. It is supplied in the natural color of the metal, protected with lacquer; other finishes can be provided by order. Adaptation may be required at the top of other flagpoles. The item is fastened by means of a lamb socket and silicone sealer.

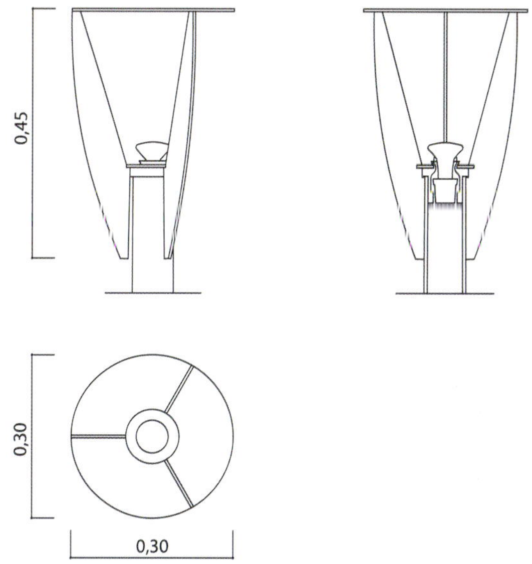

Camelot

Design: DA2

Production: Ghisamestieri

Camelot is a street lamp designed to add a familiar touch to urban spaces, with a typically interior decoration look that contrasts with its effective outdoor luminous performance. It is available in several heights and with different diffusers. These consist of an opaque anodized aluminum top designed to avoid luminous contamination, and a variety of translucent "veils" in different colors, which show up clearly in wide open spaces. The modular system allows these veils to be changed very easily, besides the possibility of using urban symmetrical or non-symmetrical luminaires. Its only support has been carefully designed so as not to interfere in the light beam at all. The available "veils" allow the most adequate style to be found for any given occasion. Camelot can be installed in any urban context, either of a contemporary or of a historical nature.

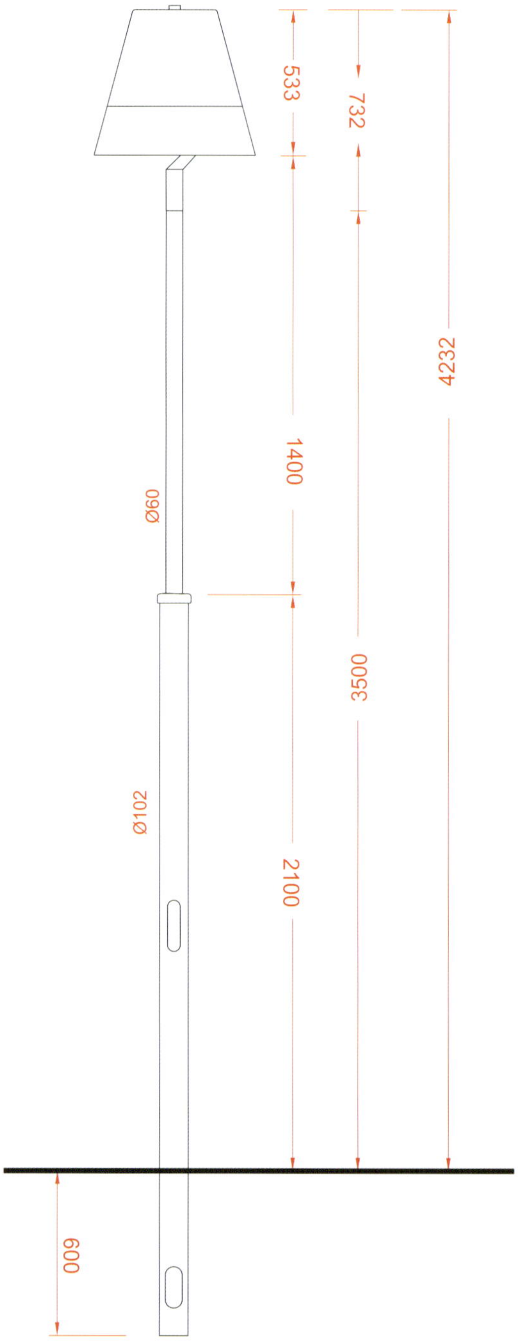

Lita

Design: Gonzalo Milà
Production: Macaedis

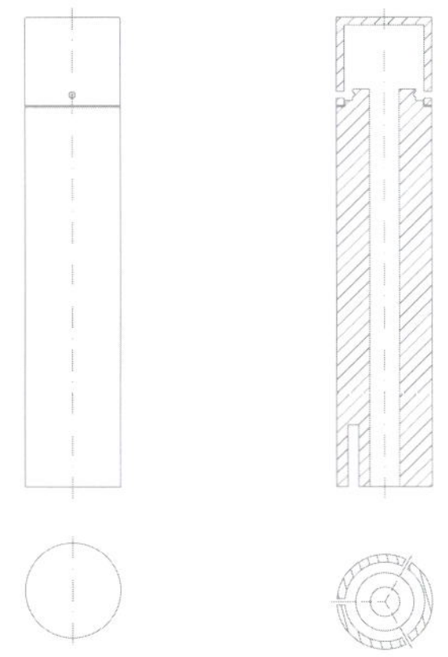

Lita is an illumination system for garden areas and paths, which consists of a cylindrical marble element that houses the fixtures and low energy light lamps of great durability. Two versions of the same model are produced, which differ in size, 160 x 500 mm (6.28 x 19.65 inches) and 160 x 800 mm (6.28 x 31.44 inches), allowing for a wider variety of installation possibilities. An innovative and unusual aspect of this product line is that the diffuser screen is made of marble, in the varieties Macael White and Macael Grey to be precise. The medium polish of the object's finish enables it to shed an amiable light with a uniquely charismatic quality. The item is designed to be anchored to the ground by means of built in corrugated rods; its weight varies between 23 and 38 kg (50.7 and 83.75 lb) according to its height.

Gabianno

Design and Production: Geohide

The Gabianno street lamp produces direct down-lighting. The luminaire accessory can be adapted onto new or existing poles of variable diameters (max. 0,24 m). The auto-stable fastening system consists of two transoms. As the article is made entirely of stainless steel, it is resistant and unalterable. The item is supplied normally with a sandblasted finish texture, but other finishes can be made available on request. It has been designed to make assembly simple and quick. The article's dimensions are: length, 3,67 m (12,03 feet); width 0,50 m (1,64 feet). The luminaire weighs 99 kg (218,196 lb).
Optional accessories are:
The c. 501 pole, with a diameter of ø 0,20 meters and a height of 10 meters (32.8 ft) above grade, made of hot-galvanized painted steel (other finishes available on request). The C. 502 extension, with a diameter of ø 0,15 meters and a height of 2,80 meters (9.18 ft) (visible) made of hot-galvanized painted steel (other dimensions and finishes on request).

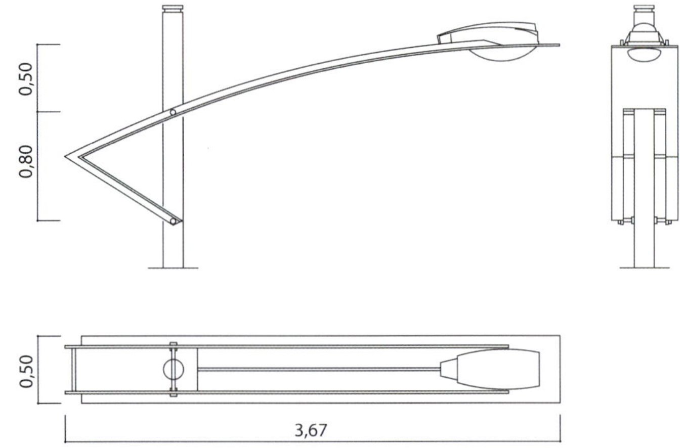

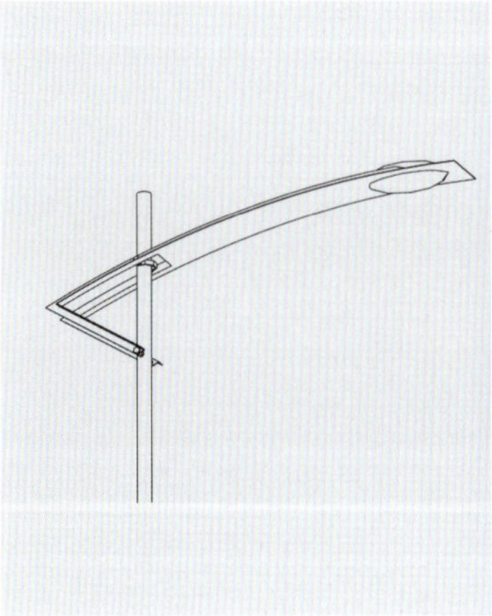

Latina

Design: Beth Galí
Production: Santa & Cole

The Latina public illumination system is an item of extraordinary visual protagonism for large urban spaces, the functional potential of which is befitting to its dimensions: it rises to a height of 15 meters (49,2 ft) and consists of three component elements, the pole, the lamp support and the tension member.
The 7 meter (22,9 ft) high pole is made of Corten steel and has three parts: a square lower segment and the remaining length which is split in two opposite halves.
The support for the luminaires is a tube of hot-galvanized steel, rectangular in cross-section, to carry five PRX-327 type lamps for discharge lamps (max. 250 W).
The tension member that provides the structure with the necessary rigidity is made of a hot-galvanized, round steel tube.
The lamp's four component parts are supplied ready for assembly: the pole, the luminaire support member, the tension member and the luminaires.
The item's total weight is 895 kg (1972,58 lb).

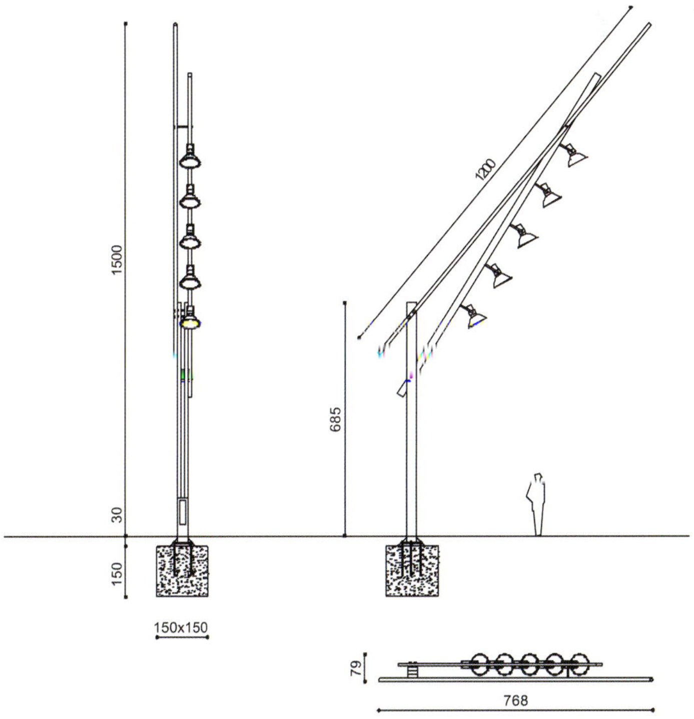

Limits

Escofet

SH

Design: David Karásek, Radek Hegmon
Production: mmcité

This radically geometrical all-steel bollard is based on a standard steel H profile, with a purely shaped top consisting of a recessed square plate.
The item consists of a galvanized steel, powder-coated body that rises 1000 mm (39,3 inches) over the pavement. It can be anchored to or under the pavement with screws.

There are several versions of the bollards, those consisting of a galvanized steel body and a cast aluminum top, as well as the all-steel models, all of which are very tough and resistant. The S-line articles are an example of the close attention this enterprise pays to even to the smallest articles of street furniture.

Vento

Design: Roger Albero
Production: DAE

The body and top of this beacon is made of cast aluminum while the shade is made of a translucent methacrylate with an outer diameter of 200mm (7.86 inches). It has a sandblasted matt anodized finish. The piece is embedded in the ground and weighs 23 kg (50.7 lb).

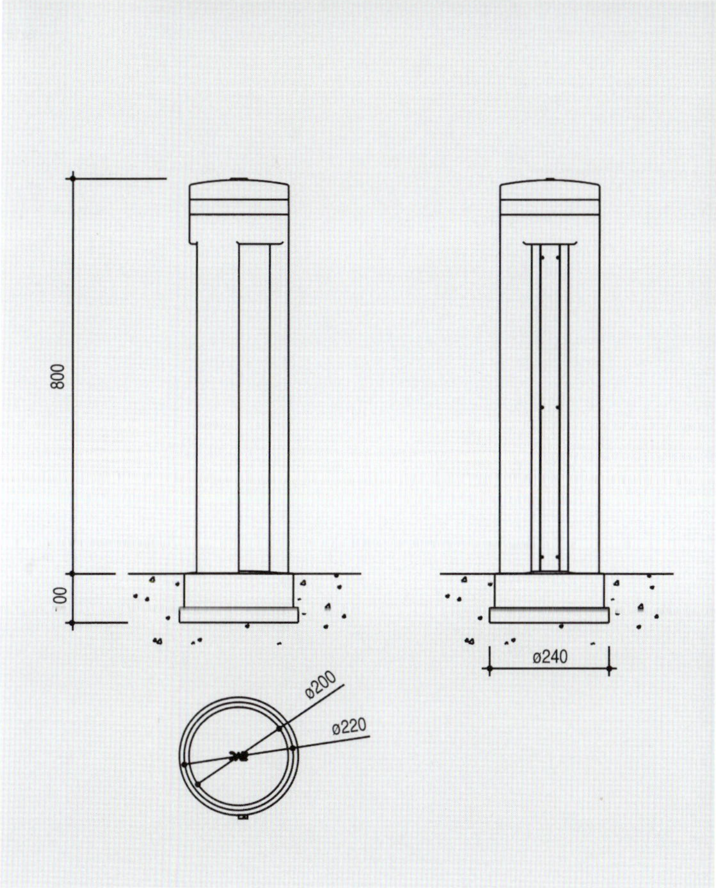

Haiku

Design: díez + díez diseño
Production: Tecnología y Diseño Cabanes

The cast iron 80cm high bollard Haiku has elegant, slender lines. The fluidity and lightness of its design is a far cry from the usual monotonous heavy bollards. Its shape is based on a triangular cross section which rotates lightly on its axis.

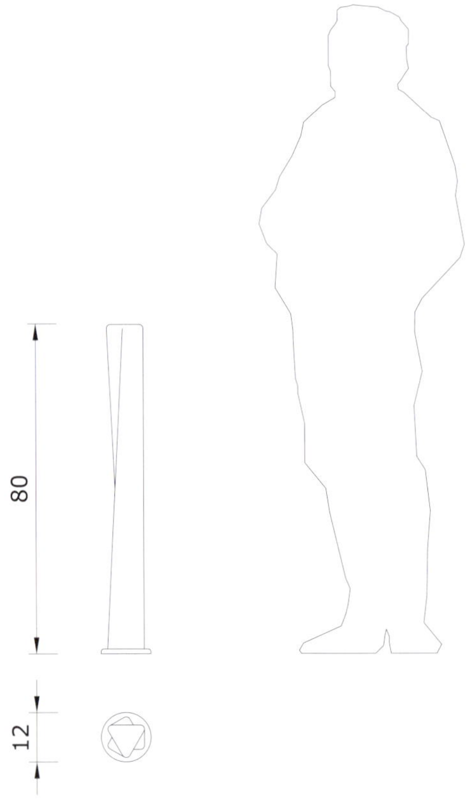

Baliza Morella

Design: Helio Piñón
Production: Escofet

This boundary post designed by Helio Piñon takes its form from two cylindrical surfaces of different radii which flow into each other, producing an object which is precise yet complex, with a misleading appearance that is visually reversible, according to whether it is hit by sunlight or whether, from twilight onwards, it is itself the projection of a low beam of light.

The Morella is much more than a boundary post and reference: it also accompanies the pedestrian. In its natural habitat in the town this is undeniably an urban piece, perhaps because of a certain complicity it has with the passers-by. Built in rust color corten steel plate each piece weighs 28 kg (61.71 lb).

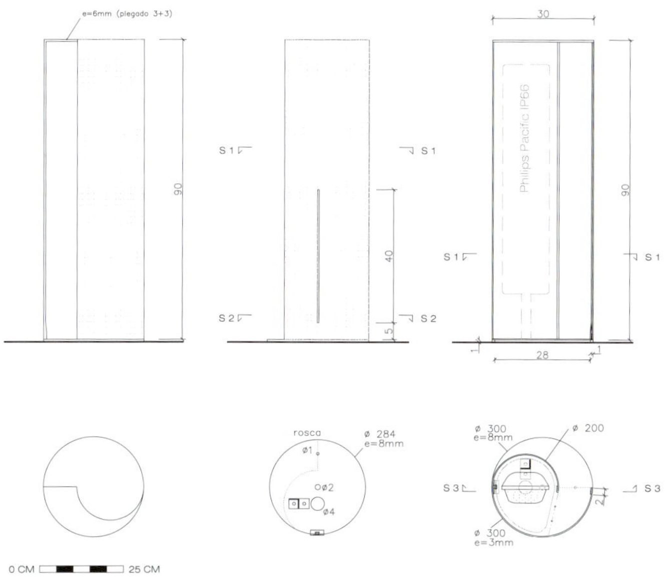

Tona

Design: Daniel Nebot
Production: Macaedis

Developed from the eccentric revolution of a truncated conoid, this piece functions as an easily visible marker for localization, contention and signaling purposes. The elimination of edges provided by this system makes this marker a very resistant element to possible aggressions. Fixing the item to the ground is achieved by a steel ring, which is anchored to the pavement and provides the cone with an elegantly finished base.
Materials: Natural stone and stainless steel.
Placing: Anchored to the ground with corrugated bars (rebars)
Size: 220 x 220 x 400 / 650 mm (8.64 x 8.64 x 15.72 / 25.54 inches)
Weight: 30 / 47 kg (66.12 / 103.58 lb)

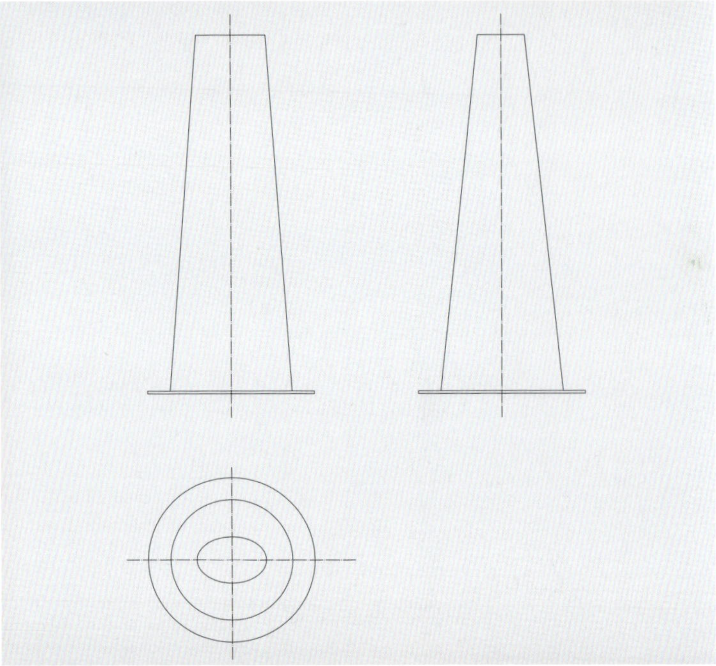

SL

Design: David Karásek, Radek Hegmon
Production: mmcité

This all-steel bollard has the most lapidary shape, which is nevertheless of notable elegance. It has been created by the simple expedient of adding a horizontal square top ending onto a standard angle-iron. This solution enables the range to include other versions of railings and even an innovative ashtray. Two dimensions are available, which can alter all the proportions of an installation: L 60 mm and L 80 mm (2.36 and 3.14 inches).

The item consists of a galvanized and powder coated steel body, which rises 1000 mm (39,3 inches) over the pavement.

There are several versions of the bollards, those consisting of a galvanized steel body and a cast aluminum top, as well as the all-steel models, all of which are very tough and resistant. The S-line articles are an example of the close attention this enterprise pays to even to the smallest articles of street furniture.

The galvanized steel profile with an aluminum alloy top (SA, SB) and the steel tube version (SC, SD, SE, SH, SL, SR) have been very successful. The new SJ range is made of cast iron. The steel elements are supplied painted in a standard color. There is an optional attachment for a connecting chain. The item is designed to be fixed to the pavement or under the pavement by concealed anchoring screws.

Luco Mojón

Design: Helio Piñón
Production: Escofet

This landmark has more image than body, more appearance than volume. Seen from the front it shows its larger size, like a cat wanting to intimidate an intruder; as you move past the object it gradually vanishes. The intention was to create an item that would naturally integrate into the city landscape without the violence generated by a new arrival, always perceived as a stranger. The object was not to be diminished but to be given a likeable configuration. Instead of the fully three-dimensional cylinder, the flatness of a spade offers the maximum visible surface to those approaching by car or on foot, but smoothly disappears as one drives or walks onward down the street. The longitudinal slot that lightens the upper half of the element provides it with an expressive gesture while providing an attaching facility for bicycles, motorcycles or dogs.

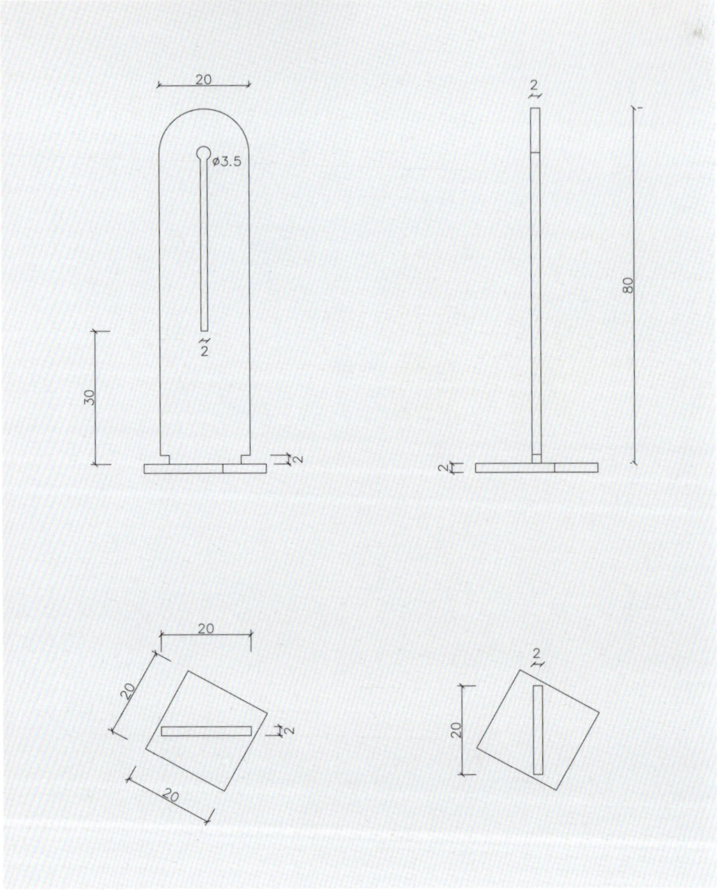

Kipp Bollard

Design: Alfred Homann
Production: Louis Poulsen

The Kipp Bollard emits symmetrical downlight. The angling of the inner diffuser together with the slightly curved design of the top shade ensures a wide and uniform distribution of light. Furthermore, the design of the internal diffuser ensures optimally even and glare-free lighting. The post is delivered in the same color as the fixture head. The fixture is phase-compensated. The article's catalogue numbers are IP55 for the fixture and IP44 for the bollard pole with access door.
The item comes with an aluminium colored textured surface finish or powder coated in grey.
The diffuser is high pressure moulded white opal acrylic. The top shade is die cast aluminum. The enclosure is injection moulded clear polycarbonate. The frame is die cast aluminum. The post, made of extruded aluminum, comes in two options: the high post and the low post; both can be installed fixed in the ground or with a base plate and screws.

Tente

Design: Leopoldo Milà
Production: DAE

The idea here is to have a flexible bollard consisting of a top, a base and a box embedded in the ground, manufactured as one piece in GG-20 pearlite cast iron. The piece can be in either polished shiny stainless steel or hot-dip galvanized steel, with a coat of high-adhesive primer, phosphocromate of polyvinyl butyral, phenoplast with rust-proof pigments, and finished with a polyester resin-based powder coating, especially for outdoor use. The standard color for this second option is wrought-iron. The approximate weight is 23.2 kg (51.13 lb). The mechanism works when the spring located in the embedded box is compressed, going into action when the piece is subjected to a pressure of 60kg (132.24 lb) or more.

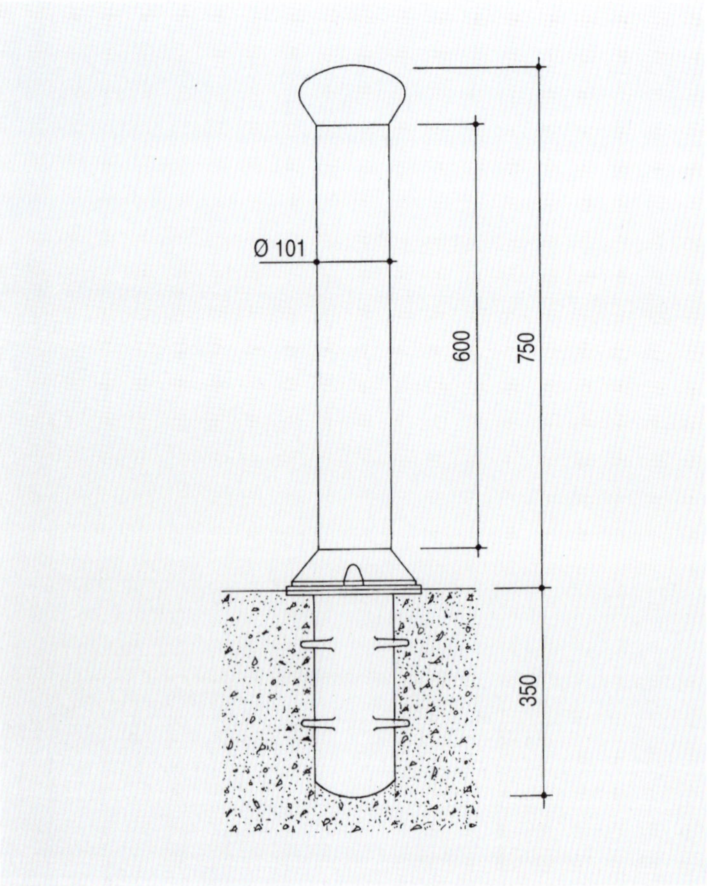

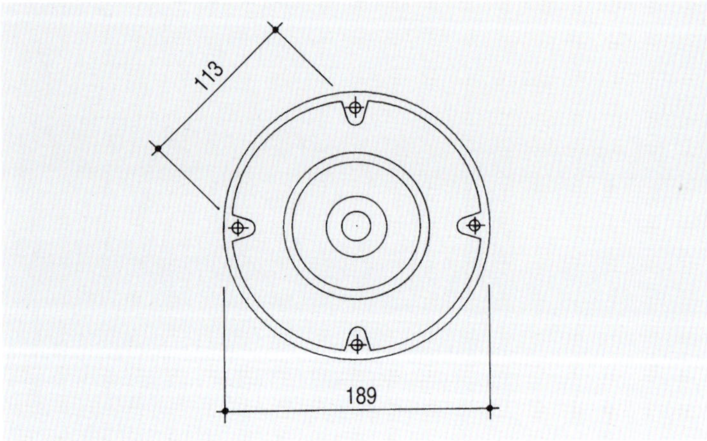

SR

Design: David Karásek, Radek Hegmon
Production: mmcité

This all-steel bollard is associated through its design and structure with the Radium benches and bin, as it works with the same see-through supporting frame made of bent steel sheet. The body is raised above the pavement upon a short leg with a base-plate.

Each bollard has a galvanized steel, powder coated body that rises 1000 mm (39,3 inches) over the pavement. It is designed to be anchored to or under the pavement with anchoring screws.

Planters

Escofet

Canasto

Design: Diana Cabeza Colors: Elisabet Cabeza
Production: Estudio Cabeza

The Canasto planter is part of a product line that consists of a large planter, a medium planter and a basket, providing a coherently integrated solution for both indoor and outdoor public spaces of a municipal, institutional, commercial or corporate nature. With a range of eight intense and luminous colors inspired in the Pre-Columbian cultures of South America and a size and volume of considerable generosity, this alternative is well suited to the dimensions and scale of these spaces. Their form and color express both the traditions, the culture and the identity of that part of the world. The material is pigmented polyethylene, formed by roto-molding and finished with a sand-blasted surface texture. The dimensions of the large model are 114 x 83 cm (44.84 x 32.62 inches) and the medium sized item measures 92 x 76 cm (36.15 x 29.86 inches).

Las Tres Damas

Design: Andreu Arriola/Carme Fiol
Production: Escofet

These planters for public areas are part of a range of urban furniture called the "The Magic Flute", inspired in the characters and in the music of Mozart's famous opera. The different urban elements of which the series consists have a unique formal character and are made of noble materials; in combination with wood and steel, a harmonious counterpoint is created between the objects, while the melodious dialogue between the objects and the neighboring urban landscape is enhanced.

The entire range of "Las tres damas" (The Three Ladies) is particularly adaptable to all sorts of urban environments, due to the multiplicity of random patterns created by the different plant species they may contain. Despite the choice of Corten steel as the construction material, the shapes revert to the traditional forms of traditional pottery plant containers, to which toughness and wear-proof durability are added, as public urban furniture requires. These planters are the ideal containers for the floral tone of a musical dialogue that can be made to arise in the streets of the city.

Femina

Design: Òscar Tusquets Blanca
Production: Macaedis

The Femina planter is a sophisticated marble container out of which the plants emerge through an elegantly scrolled gap between the two halves of the top cover, allowing the necessary space for the stem or the trunk of the plant to grow. The independence between the exterior object and the container inside it make it easy to change or renovate the soil or the type of vegetation; maintenance is also reduced to the minimum. The Femina planter's cubical volume is available in three different sizes and in several varieties of marble, including Travertine Red, Travertine Cream, Macael White, Macael Yellow and Macael Cream.

Arcadia

Design: díez+díez diseño

This image corresponds to the award winning project in the First Public Space Design Competition organized by CTAP (Centro Tecnológico Andaluz de la Piedra: Andalusian Stonework Technological Center).

The project aimed to generate a program for the creation of urban spaces that go beyond the mere definition of the items of public furniture, to become a defining factor of the location. The image shows us an example of a tree planter that blends into the pavement which it is an integral part of. Emulating the typical protuberances of the terrain that arise around the foot of a tree, in this case a further protuberance appears in the form of a welcoming seat, which seems to be just another random incidental of the surrounding landscape.

Casicilíndrica

Design: Gonzalo Milà - Martina Zink
Production: Santa & Cole

Three plant stands with simple shapes to adorn urban sidewalks. Their different capacities allow for a wide variety of plantings.
Presented in three sizes with different diameters and heights. The plant stand is made of a single piece of cast iron with anti-rust protection, painted dark-grey. The element is simply positioned onto the ground. No maintenance required.
Weights:
Ø 1,00m: 226 kg (Ø 3.28 ft: 498 lb)
Ø 0,80m: 150 kg (Ø 31.44 inches: 330.6 lb)
Ø 0,55m: 121 kg (Ø 21.61 inches: 266.68 lb)

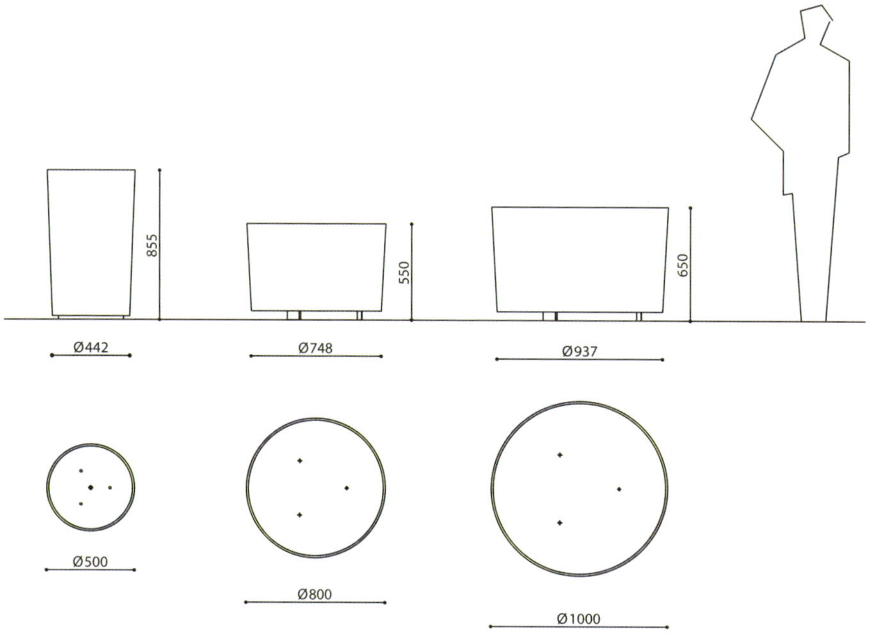

Cestae

Design: Silvia López
Production: Macaedis

Both the name and the physical appearance of this solidly constructed planter read as an allusion to the aesthetic ambiance of classical Rome. Constructed out of four powerful slabs of stone, the item presents an image of unquestionable solidity within the urban context. The high quality resolution of the joins and the simplicity of the outline make this a pleasingly versatile item to choose, which can be fitted into traditional or more contemporary environments. The Cestae planters are available in the following types of fine marble: Alhambra Yellow, Eneus, White Macael, Green Macael, Golden Travertine, Iberian Cream, Marquina Black, as well as Capri Limestone. The article's dimensions are 600 x 600 x 550 mm (23.58 x 23.58 x 21.61 inches), with an interior capacity of 245 liters (8.65 ft^3) and a total weight (when empty) of 160 kg (352.64 lb), due to which the only installation needed is to place it in the correct chosen location.

Morella

Design: Helio Piñón
Production: Escofet

The name of the Morella series derives from a commission received from the urban planning office of that locality, and the brief to create a solvently constructed, formally coherent series of urban elements with a manifestly genuine character. To achieve the desired quality, resistance to wear and natural appearance, Corten steel was chosen as the main material: The series is made to last both visually and materially, making it a suitable choice to furnish public spaces with permanent facilities of an aesthetic nature, yet avoiding alien decorative statements that might disrupt the existing contextual environment. These items are well-suited to historic sites, where textures and atmospheres generated by superimposed cultures and periods cannot be interfered with lightly and where the placement of extraneous elements requires the conjunction of high quality and a low profile.

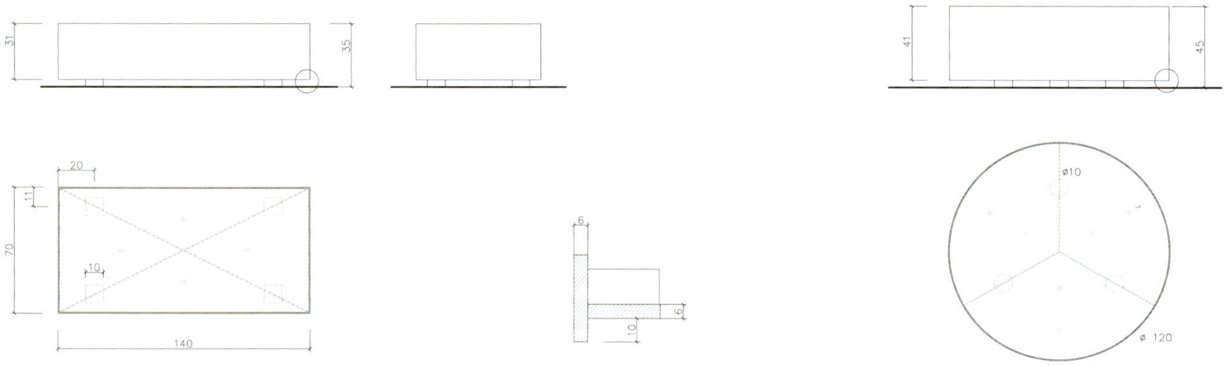

Barcina

Design: Jaume Bach - Gabriel Mora
Production: Fundició Dúctil Benito

This planter has become established as a constant presence throughout the urban context of the city of Barcelona. It is a sturdy piece of public furniture conceived as a suitable inclusion into any sort of environment, with a formal appearance that makes a classical, deeply-rooted statement. The choice of an exceptionally durable material such as cast iron guarantees the "Barcina" planter its optimal resistance to any sort of erosion, thereby minimizing the maintenance budget correspondingly. The simple yet elegant circular bowl rests upon three spherical feet. One of these is perforated to drain away excess water while permitting the bowl's balance to be adjusted to the possible inclination of the pavement.

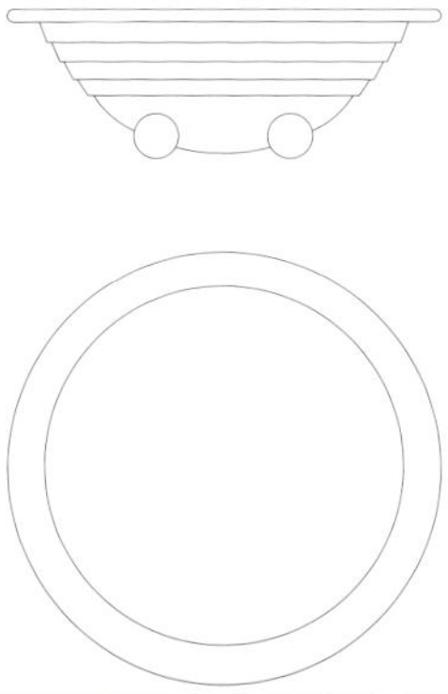

Beach elements

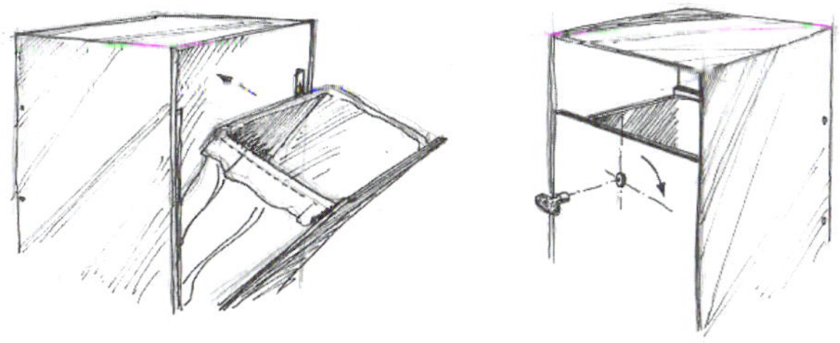

Lavapiés

Design: José Luis Camarasa
Production: Santa & Cole

The foot-shower designed by José Luis Camarasa has a system that works like a public drinking fountain, except that it flows downwards, through 10 independently worked outlets of needle-spray water nozzles. The structure consists of a polished stainless steel (AISI 316) tube, Ø 200 mm in diameter (7.86 inches), supported upon pillars of the same material but with a sandblasted finish. The internally concealed spray nozzles are made of brass and the press-button to release the flow is of stainless steel. The platform at the base of the structure is a galvanized steel grid that enables the water and the unwanted sand to drain away instantly and perfectly.
The article is connected to the mains through one of the supporting pillars. The body can be opened at both ends to facilitate maintenance work, which is minimal as the entire article is constructed using resistant, non-alterable materials. The foot-shower is ergonomically designed for people to clean the sand off their feet with the maximum comfort and security.

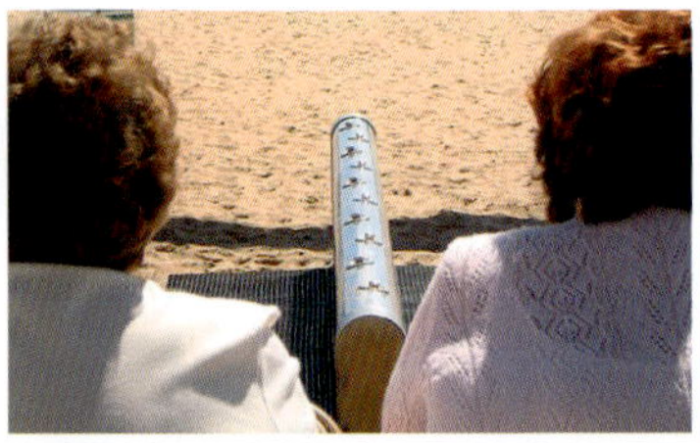

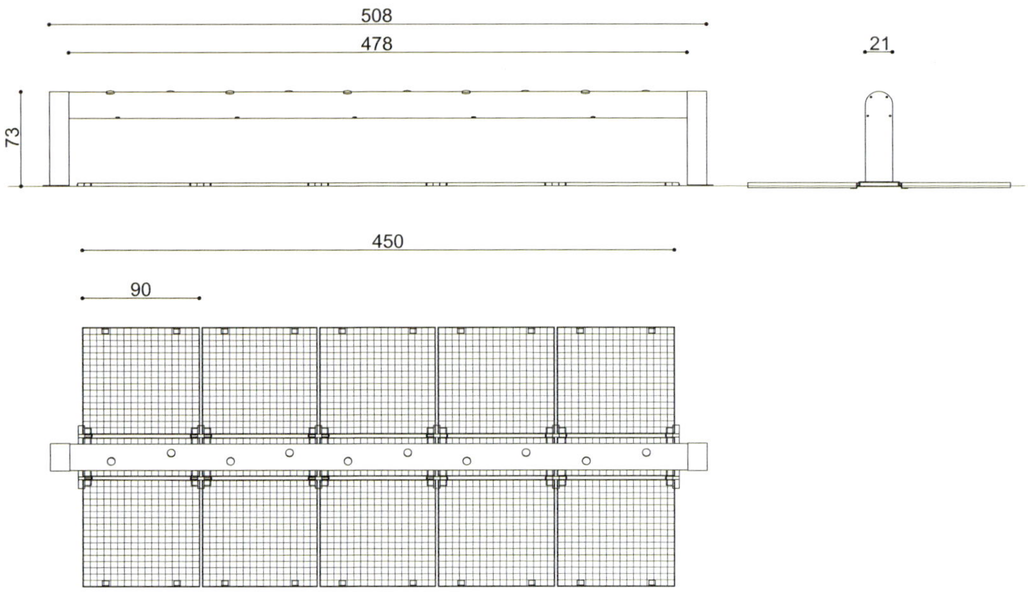

Apoios de Praia

Design: Alcino Soutinho
Production: Larus

These pieces are intended for the catering industry, to support activities on the beach during the summer season. They are modular elements which provide a bar unit complete with its counter, a unisex bathroom with access for the disabled and a third module for a medical service. The main structure and the roof are constructed in marine board coated on both sides with fiberglass reinforced polyester resin, and include a thermal insulation of polyurethane foam. The ensemble sits on a stainless steel structure. The flooring consists of a non-slip plywood board in the bar area and a non-slip aluminum overlay in the bathroom and medical area.

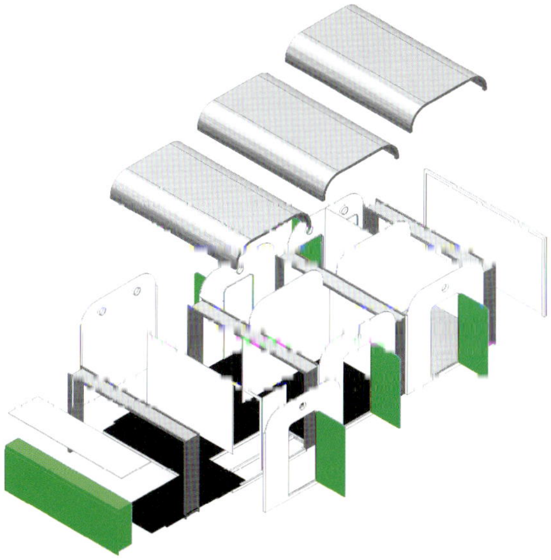

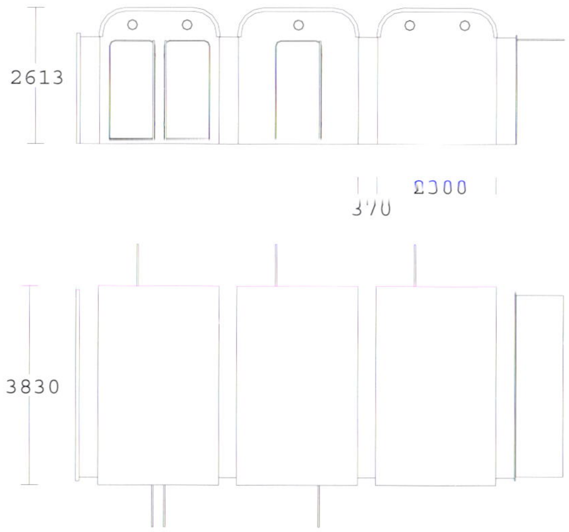

Bina

Design: Gonzalo Milà - Martina Zink - Área Metropolitana de Barcelona
Production: Santa & Cole

In collaboration with the MMAMB (Mancomunidad de Municipios del Área Metropolitana de Barcelona; Associated Municipalities of the Barcelona Metropolitan Area), Gonzalo Milà and Martina Zink designed this litter bin to solve the problem of litter-collection on the beach. Functional and elegant, it meets all the requirements of popular beach resorts: large capacity, low maintenance, quickly removable, a lock against vandalism and firm placement, as the lower 30 cm, buried in the sand, are filled with sand before the plastic bag is placed inside. The bins can be stacked for easy storage in the winter. The pigmented polypropylene body permits personalization or adaptation to the surroundings. The lid includes a space for a name, logo or municipal coat of arms to be engraved.
The body and lid are made of rotomolded pigmented polypropylene and weigh 10.40 kg (23 lb). The rounded lid has a central hole. The neck of the body is designed for easy placement of the bag, which remains concealed once the lid is closed. The bin has a capacity of 165 liters; it is 1.22 meters (4 ft) high but the lower 30 cm (1 ft) are buried in the sand, so it only stands 0.92 cm (3 ft.) high upon the sand. The upper diameter is 63 cm (2,06 ft) and the lower diameter, at sand level, measures 45 cm (1,47 ft.). A special lever to open it is provided with the bin, which is delivered fully assembled, but with assembly instructions. Zero maintenance is required.

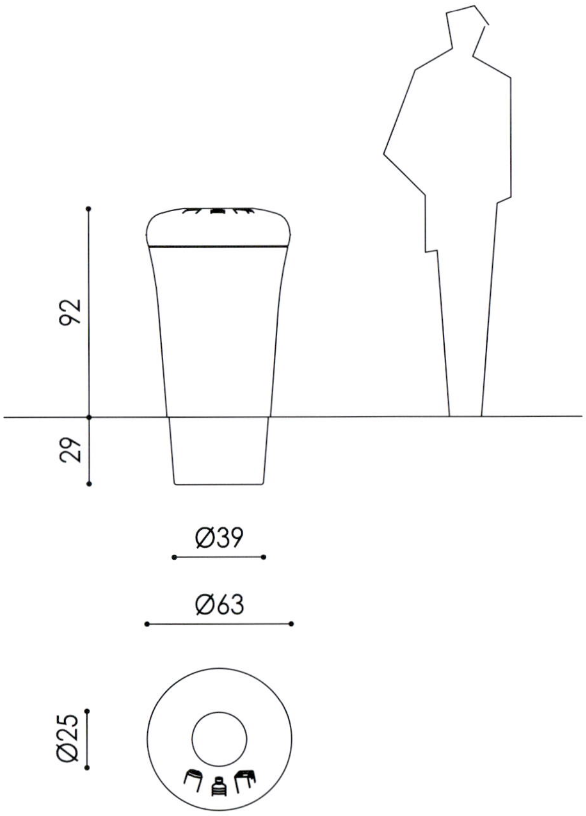

Pass

Design: Jordi Miralles Tintoré, Jordi Miró Surroca
Production: mago: urban

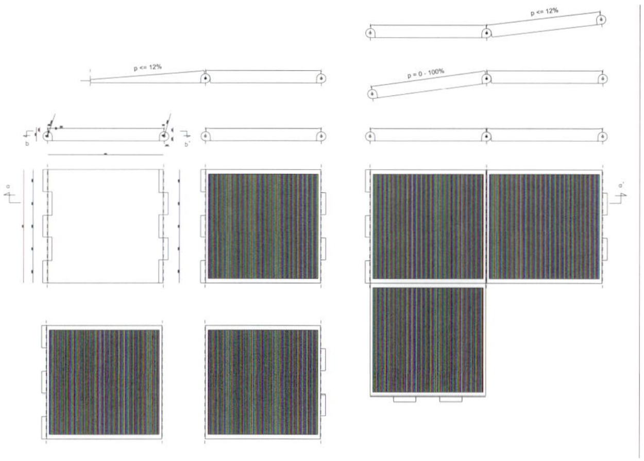

Up until now, getting to the shore involved walking over the sand with no other protection than your sandals, or along a more or less irregular platform with a potential risk of falling. Moreover, the lack of an appropriate end made it difficult for people in wheelchairs or with limited mobility to get to the water.

To address these problems, mago: urban came up with the Pass platform, which consists of a line of juxtaposed modular slabs of reinforced concrete. The slabs are square, the upper side is flat and two of its sides are smooth; the third side has three convex teeth and two concave indentations, which permits the modules to be hooked onto each other.

The teeth and the indentations have a cylindrical perforation for the units to be locked together with a steel rod. This hinge mechanism allows the system enough flexibility to adapt to the terrain without affecting its smoothness and comfort.

The Pass module's upper face is entirely textured with anti-slip corrugations. Special modules are available for each end, where a smoothly tapered edge makes the platform easily accessible for all users.

An extra facility added by mago:urban to their Pass platform is the joining mechanism is functional on three sides, so a perpendicular platform may be connected to the main path. All the modules and the resulting walkway can be anchored to the ground, but only require their own weight and collective structure for stability.

Ada

Design and Production: Microarquitectura

Designed for seaside or outdoor use, this series of items consists of a shower, a foot-shower, a drinking fountain and a waste-basket. Each item has two sides that can be embossed, engraved or otherwise personalized to conform to the characteristics of a given location or municipality.
The shower consists of a compact self supporting pillar that contains the entire plumbing system inside it. It is adapted for use by handicapped people. Its main components (the pillar and the platform) as well as the rest of the accessories have been conceived as separate entities. One single column can carry up to four separate shower nozzles, two for regular showering and two for the feet or the very small.
The foot-shower is vandal-proof. It is made of stainless steel with side covers of HPL; it is supplied with a double nozzle and a timer. The Ada drinking fountain,

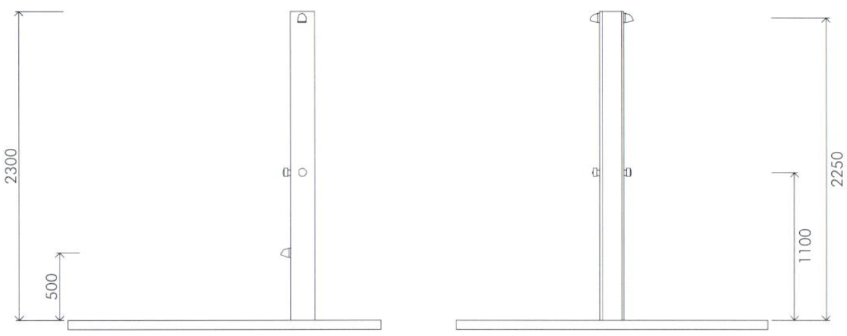

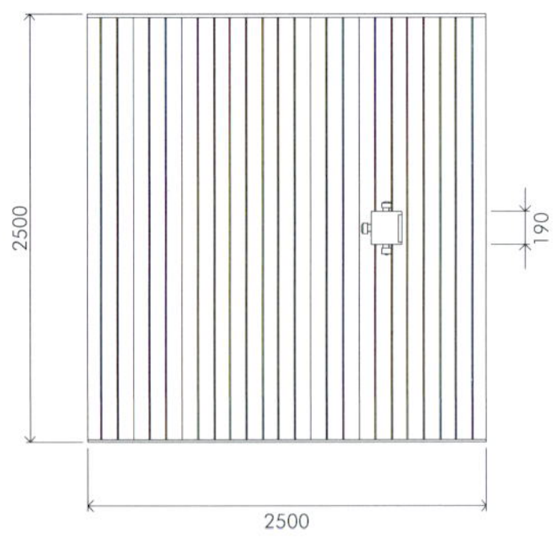

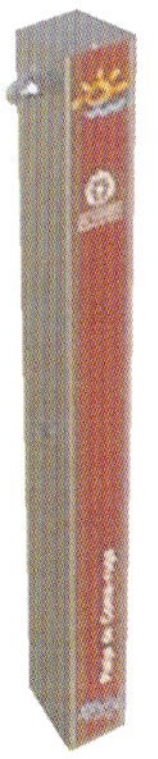

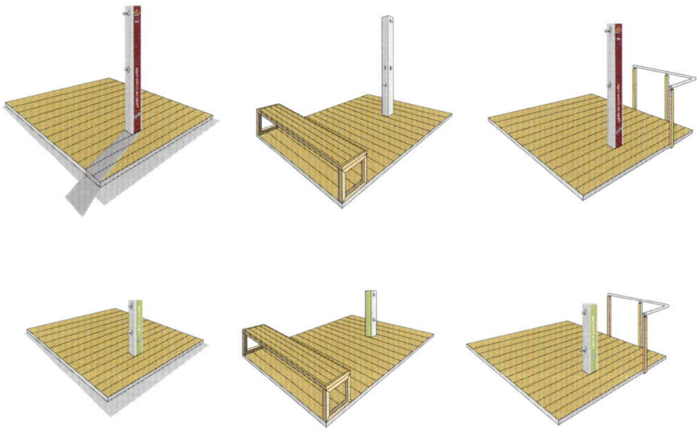

made of the same materials as the foot-shower, has the nozzle in one of the sides and a timer operated press-button. Finally, the wastebasket is a rectangular volume measuring 40 x 40 cm (15.72 x 15.72 inches) wide and 1 m (3,28 ft) in height, although there is a model 2 m (6,56 ft) high that doubles its function as a sign bearer. The concept and the materials implemented for this series make it optimally resistant and easy to personalize.

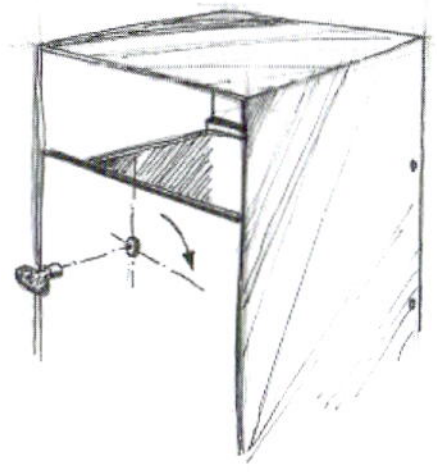

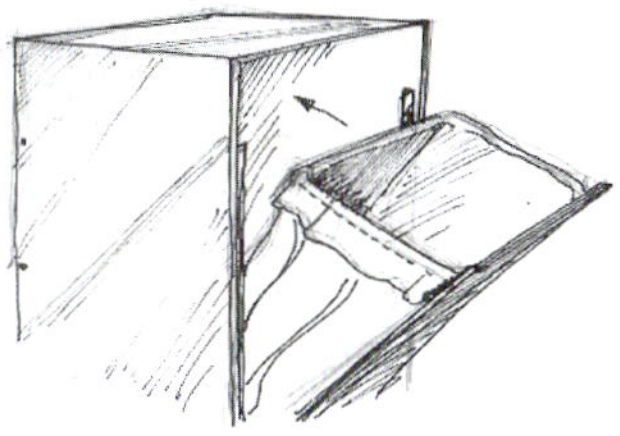

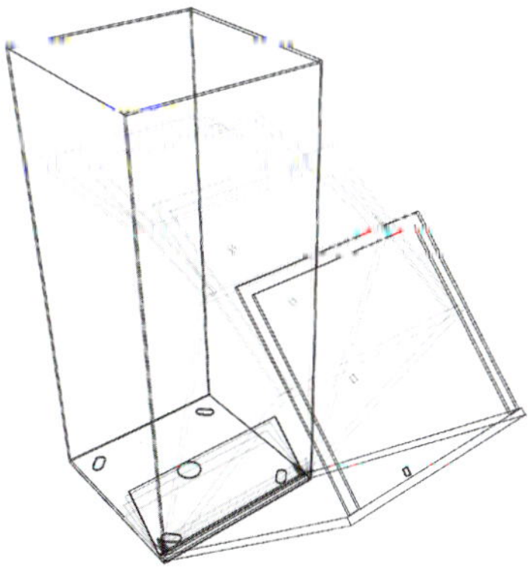

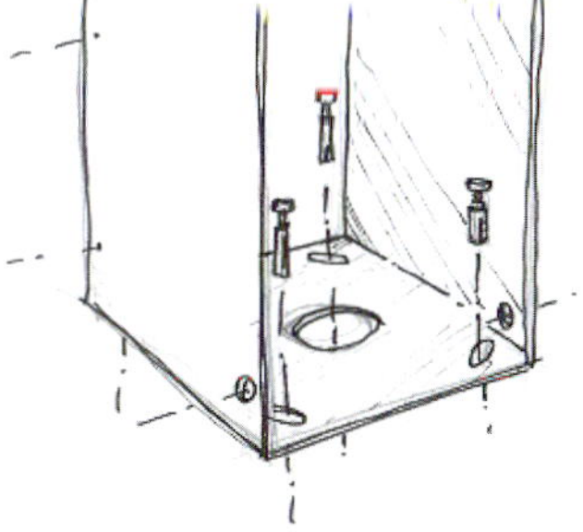

Games

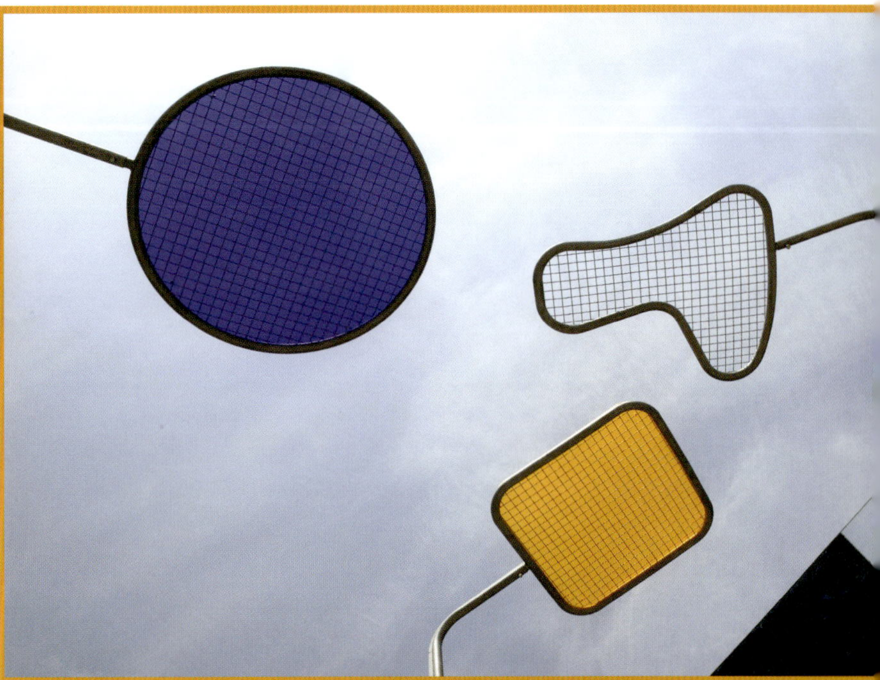

Trottola

Design: Mitzi Bollani
Production: Modo

Trottola is a soft, round children's game that is reminiscent of an old-fashioned spinning top. As well as providing a game for children, it also takes on a purely aesthetic value when placed in a square or green area.
Pleasing to the eye, Trottola offers a creative, more personalized way of sitting down for both the young and the elderly. Due to its unusual shape, it can accommodate a number of people who can position themselves in different ways. This is particularly good for children, who like to try out new postures and will enjoy the freedom of movement.
The different possible inclinations allow it to offer a comfortable seat to the elderly because, being a little higher than usual, it is not necessary to make an effort to stand up again; at the same time, a child could easily sit down on the lower part.
This element meets different requirements in a creative and innovative way, with respect for people's needs and ages and with an eye to aesthetic value.

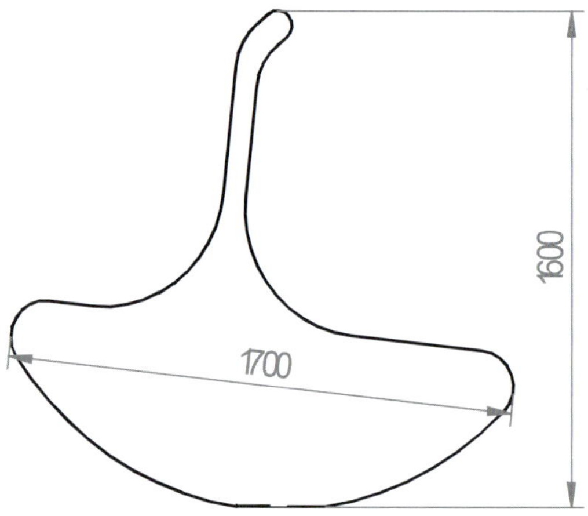

Bibornes

Design and Production: Geohide

This item consists of a system of bollards or information poles designed to attract passers by, transmitting information in the form of a game. Suitable for indoor or outdoor installation, the communication game is based on the loudhailer principle, involving at least 2 participants and 2 bollards, each with an incorporated loudhailer component. The flexible tube connecting the two elements does not require any electrical or mechanical devices. There are mobile plaques with an attachment for interchangeable informative texts or questionnaires, adapted to all languages and ages (didactic and recreational circuits in tourist towns, parks, zoos, museums, kindergartens, etc...) The circular platform serves as step. The anchoring pretube, designed to be embedded in the ground or the pavement, is made of hot-dip-galvanized steel. Optionally, the items can be delivered with a lacquered paint finish, in a range of standard tones (color as requested).

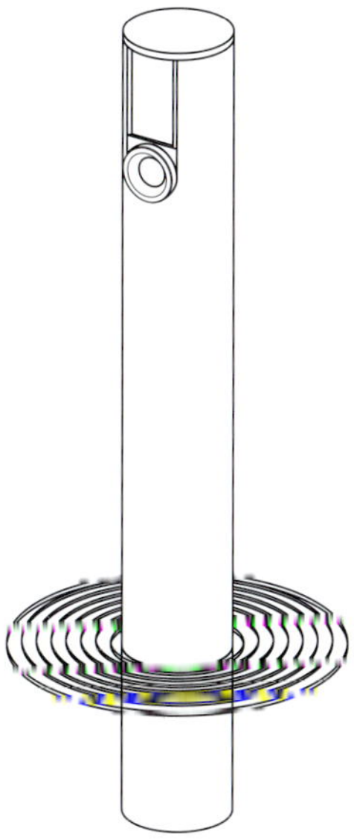

Organo di Pan

Design: Tobia Repossi
Production: Modo

A game consisting of an arrangement of stainless steel tubes of varying heights, which produce sounds with different tonalities. But this is just on first impression. Listening more closely reveals that the structure produces more than just sounds and notes - there are also vibrations, frequencies and resonances that can turn out to be familiar.
The tube structure includes various diameters: they can be 30mm, 40mm or 48mm, and they rise up out of the ground to a considerable height.
As well as aiming to provide a musical element in relation to children's games, the Organo di Pan is also aesthetically musical, resembling a huge instrument somewhat like an organ, a xylophone or even a harp.

Mowgli

Design: Antoni Roselló Til
Production: Esteva

There is a primal relationship between children and trees. To scramble up or down, climb, hang upside down or change levels are basic, immediate actions. A large cylinder (trunk) acts as a support for various tubular elements arranged in a seemingly spontaneous way (branches) make up the basic conceptual configuration of this game.

It is easy to set up, allowing the elements to be placed in various different ways, either in a disordered and anarchic fashion or in ordered groups.

The proximity of the poles and branches suggest a forest and create a kind of net that allows children to move as though through a jungle, without touching the ground, in a playful and exclusive space.

Materials: Stainless steel and molded iroko wood.

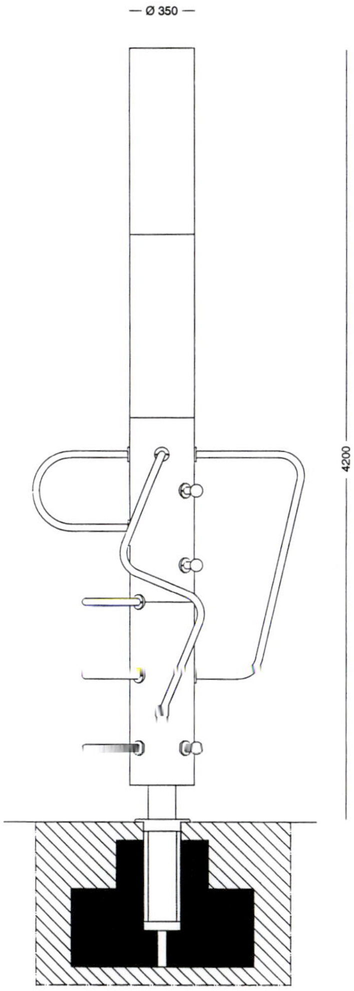

Shadow Play

Design: Ana Mir-Emili Padrós / Emiliana Design Studio
Production: Richter Spielgeräte

Shadow Play is an interactive educational game that allows users/children to control and superimpose shapes and colors of sunlight reflected on the ground. It is also an element of street furniture that creates shaded points in open areas that are exposed to the sun.

Shadow Play consists of a pole anchored to the ground (adaptable to any kind of surface) and a 360º rotating element on the top that is opaque or translucent and produces the shadows on the ground. The minimum recommended composition is three heights of Shadow Play (4.4, 4.2and 4.0 meters / 14.43, 13.77 and 13.12 feet), allowing shapes and colours to overlap.

There are five panel designs that offer various combinations: numbers, letters, opaque shapes, translucent colors, eclipse effects....and they can even be exclusively designed to the client's specifications.

The upper panel is turned through a handle/wheel, which is designed to conceal the rotation joint in order to avoid children hurting themselves and prevent vandalism. The design also protects the mechanism from inclement weather and from users climbing the pole. The upper joint is also reinforced in order to prevent damage from vandalism.

All the metal parts are stainless steel with a matte finish and the translucent elements are highly weatherproof methacrylate.

Distorting Mirror

Design: Tobia Repossi
Production: Modo

The distorting mirror game consists of a square tubular structure of 40x40 mm (1,57x1,57 inches) AISI 304 stainless steel tubing, covered with an AISI 304 stainless steel mirror-finished reflecting panel, 2 mm (0,078 inches) thick, curved according to the visual distortion criteria. Two different versions of the distorting mirrors are available: High-Short or Fat-Thin. Both are provided with base-plates to be fixed onto a concrete slab with four M8 nogs and buried 200 mm (7,86 inches) underground (to be arranged beforehand and not included in our supply). On request, prefabricated concrete plinths can be supplied, to be buried at the same depth. All these articles are tested and approved by the Italian Toy Safety Institute, according to the UNI EN 1176 regulations. This approval is confirmed by the application of the Tested safety Label.

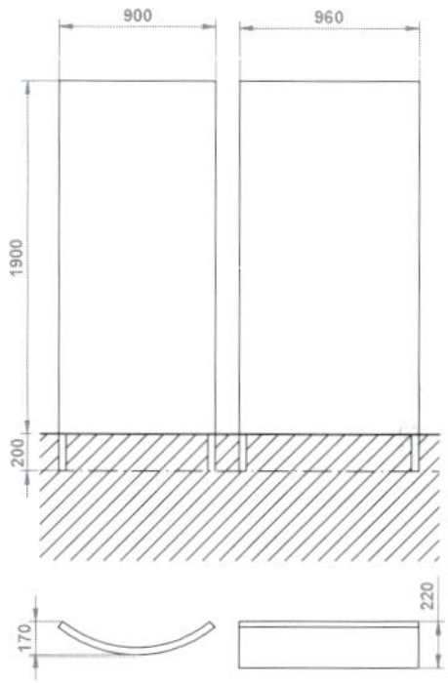

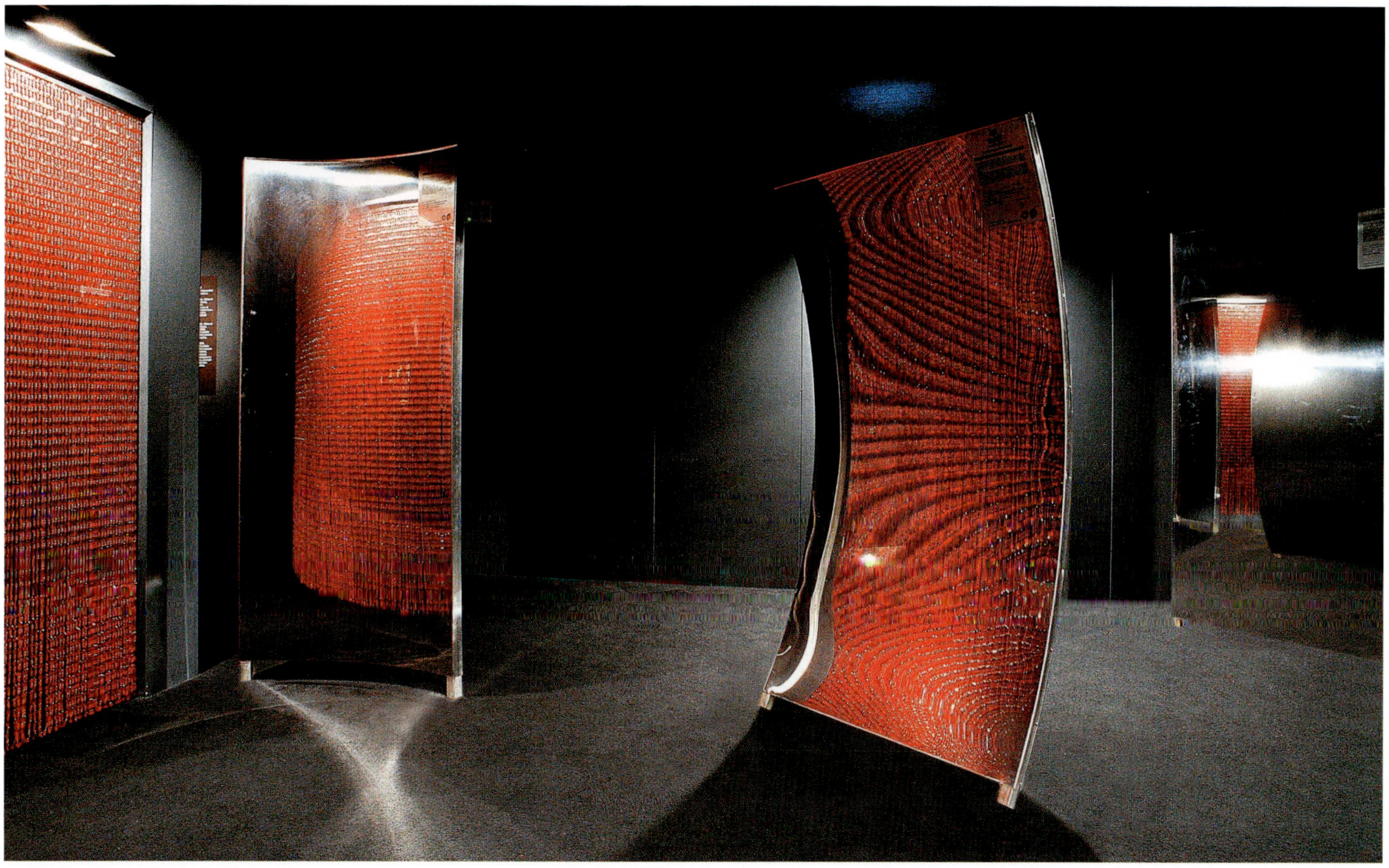

Floors

Pictorical pavements

Design: Antoni Roselló Til
Production: Santa & Cole

The pictorial pavement series is a tribute to four artists who changed our perception of image: Henry Matisse, Piet Mondrian, Vassily Kandinsky and Paul Klee. They give art a functional urban use, applying it to pavements, an element remained unchanged since the XIX century. Inspired by pictorial tree-base grids, Antoni Roselló developed these pavings intending to integrate art into daily urban life environment, without troubling it, not as an alien but rather as a functional element. In a personal tribute to each painter, the elements of the series bear the name of each one of them, while the tree grids bear his family name; this allows for a great combination of pavements and tree-base grids. With these interesting pieces, Santa & Cole brings focus onto an element considered to be the skin of the city, the base of any future urban development. The concrete tiles take on the negative or positive image of each of the four painters, while functionally reinforcing the sidewalk. The pictorial pavement series satisfies the need to incorporate symbols into urban furniture, gives an iconographic value to urban space, and contributes to the city's identity.

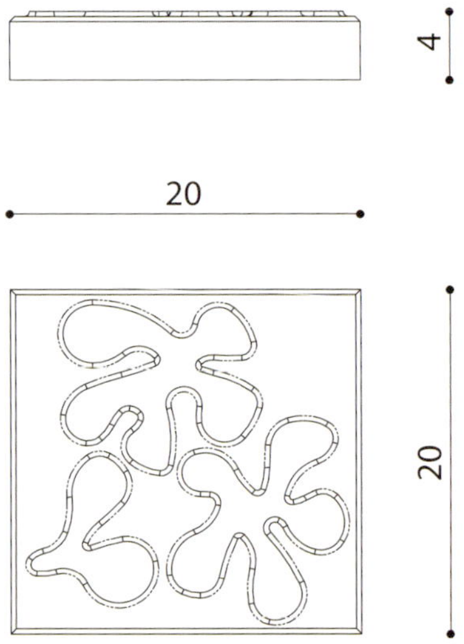

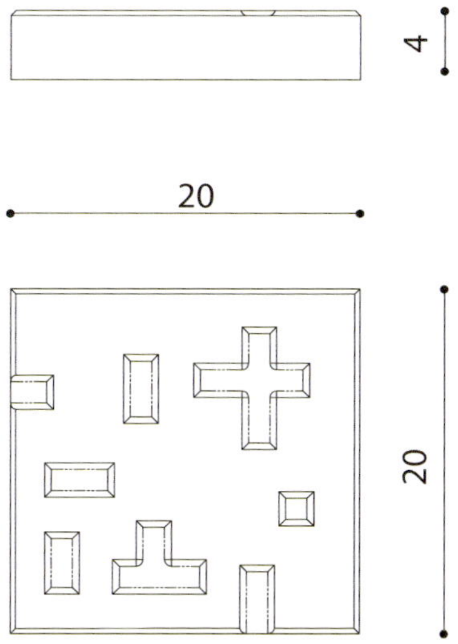
4
20
20

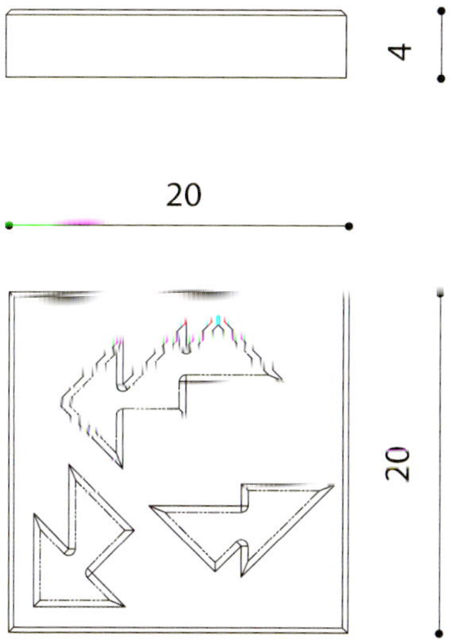
4
20
20

Chequerblock

Design: Hastings Pavement Company License New York
Production: Escofet

Checkerblock is a paving stone made out of vibrated and molded reinforced concrete in squares of 610 x 610 x 100 mm (24 x 24 x 3.93 inches). It is ideal for landscaping an area in concrete and grass, as it lets you shape the land and at the same time prevent erosion, performing like a reinforcement of vegetation and planted areas. The final appearance, with the grass growing between the gaps, is particularly attractive and visually pleasing. This combination of a green layer mixed with the solidity of a concrete surface is reassuring. The product comes in various colors, with a fine, smooth surface texture and it is laid over compacted sand. Each weighs 38 kg (83.75 lb).

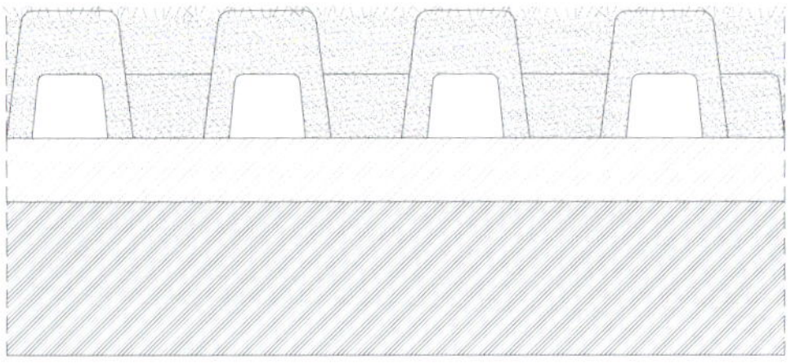

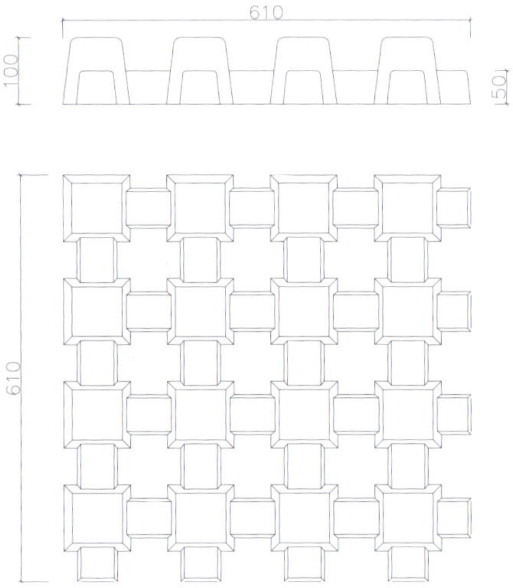

Palma

Design: J.A Martínez Lapeña / Elías Torres

Production: Escofet

Palma paving stones are available in two formats that allow them to form different systems of drainage pavements, leaving the joints more or less open to silting with sand or to grasses appearing in the gaps.

The Palma x 2 is a piece that doubles the size of the original Palma paving stone, opening up the possibility of combinations forming endless compositions. The original paving will be defined by factors like the variations in the joints, the direction in which they are geometrically placed and the way the two sizes are set.

Suitable for zones with pedestrian traffic and the occasional vehicle, both formats are 10cm thick. When they are placed, the paving stones are pressed into a bed of sad with a granulation grading of 1-5 and a thickness of 3 to 5cm, laid over a base of compacted gravel or a 15cm concrete base with a characteristic resistance of 250 kg/cm^2.

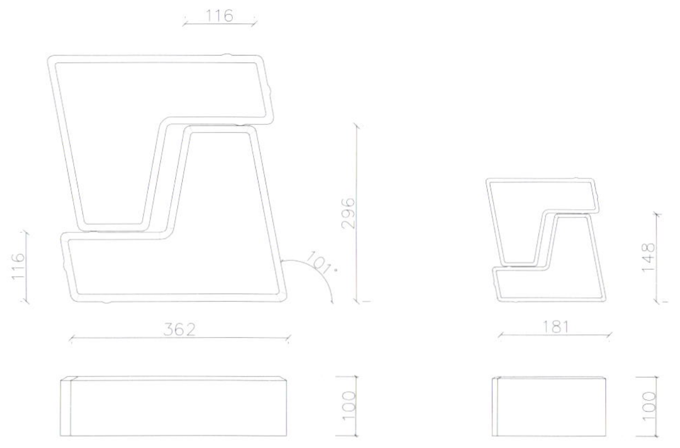

Bus shelters

Foster

Design: Norman Foster
Production: JC Decaux

This bus shelter has been chosen for the Champs Elyseés in Paris. With a double sided lateral enclosure, it has a capacity for eighteen people, including seating for five or six. The overall design combines glass and steel for maximum visual and formal lightness, while also offering maximum protection from meteorological elements at either end. The vertical structure has been reduced to its most essential elements, and the design of the roof support elements, as well as the suspended bench, seem to follow the designer's high tech aesthetic.

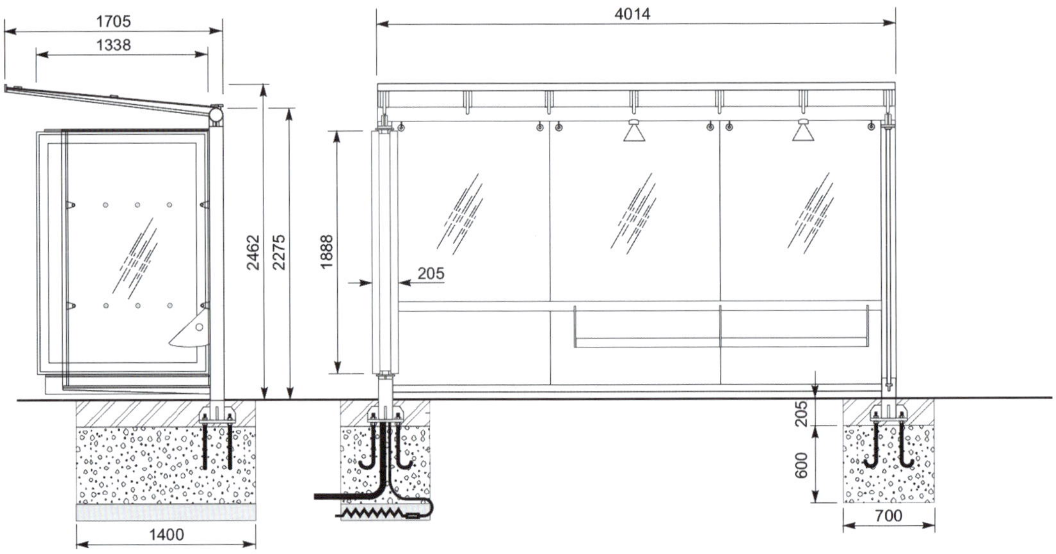

Gull Wing

Design: Brunetti Filipponi associati
Production: Ora Centurelli

The supporting structure of the Gullwing bus stop shelter consists of 2 hot-galvanized steel tubular bars, with a round cross-section of 100 x 2 mm (3,93 x 0,08 inches). There are base-plates and backing plates at each end, provided with log bolts to bury in the reinforced concrete foundation slab.
The item comes complete with a roof shelter of galvanized steel sheet (thickness 10/10). (0,39 x 0,39 inches).
Double walls are available on request for advertising and/or lighting purposes. There are provisions for a bench (size 1700 x 400 mm) (67,49 x 15,88 inch) and a litter bin. All iron parts are hot-galvanized, according to UNI regulations. RAL paint coating is an optional choice. This prestigious product is ideal for any environment.

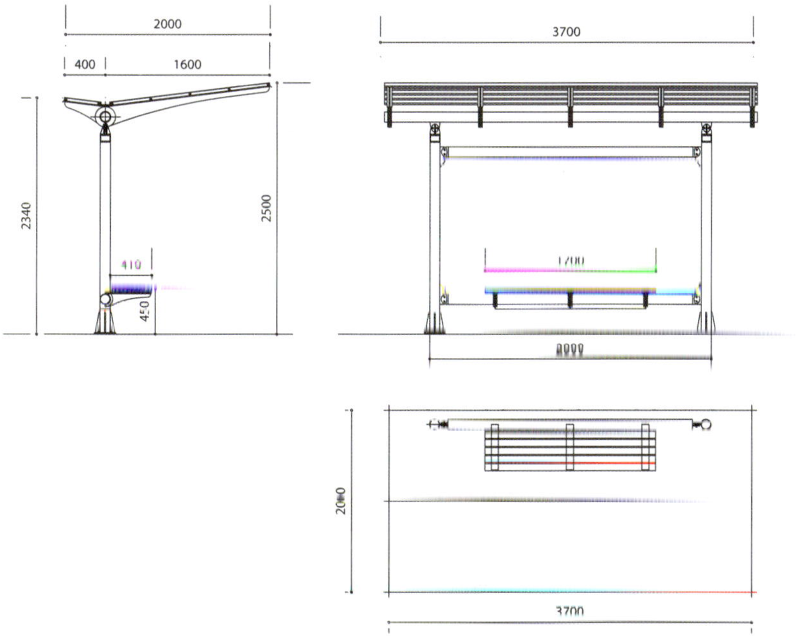

BMG

Design: David Karásek, Radek Hegmon
Production: mmcité

With the supporting structure situated in the rear wall, the simple and clear design of this bus stop shelter is based on the combination of big glass areas, the coarse galvanized surfaces of the supporting steel parts and the powder coated frame details. The glass roof is provided with sand stripes, to filter the direct sunlight inside the shelter. The rear wall is hung on the frame from outside. The side walls can perform as backlit show-cases (CLV) to carry advertising, maps of the city or any other graphic information. They can also be enclosed in clear or mirror glass. This modern shelter designed for the city of Brno certifies its qualities in all types of city areas including historic centers.
The structure consists of rough finished galvanized steel with powder coated details. Tempered glass encloses the roof, back wall and sides. Rain water drains through one of the pillars. The solid wooden seat is treated for outdoor use. For narrow locations, an optional model with no side walls is also available.

Buenos Aires

Design: Diana Cabeza, Leandro Heine, Martín Wolfson Graphic Design: Osvaldo A. Ortiz, D.G. Gabriela Falgion, D.G. Pablo Cosgaya - D.G. Marcela Romer Engineering: Alberto Fainstein, Mauro Galli

The project to install these bus shelters is currently in process through a contract for the Buenos Aires city government, which includes shelters, shelter systems, public transport stops, public transport transfer centres, urban signage, benches and bicycle parking facilities. This bus shelter has a light, contemporary design thanks to the extensive use of transparent elements and the configuration of the elements that form the support structure. As well as protecting bus users, the slightly curved roof element also protects the shelter structure itself, the advertising panel and the litter bins. The curve shape is repeated in the back wall, providing shelter on the reverse side in the case of rain or wind.

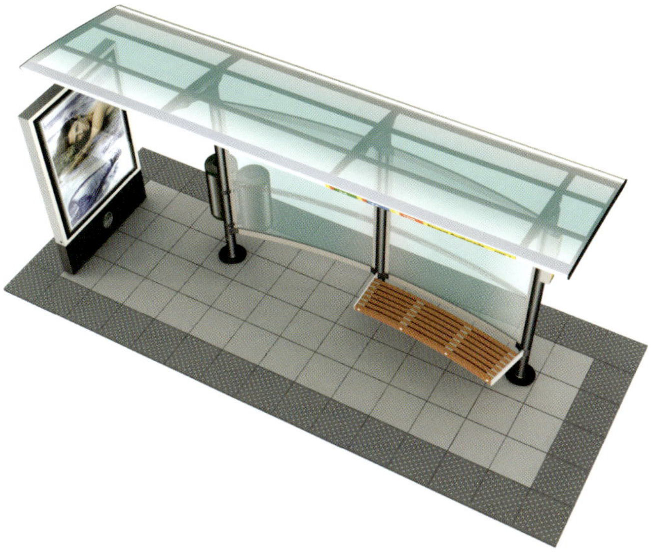

Tokay

Design: Lisa Segatori
Production: ORA Centurelli

The main structural frame of the Tokay bus stop shelter is made of n°2 galvanized steel sheet sides with a thickness of 3 mm, made by plasma technology. The pierced decoration can be customized, thereby adapting the character of the item to different architectural contexts, from the classical to the severely contemporary. The whole skeleton is made of electrically welded square steel tubing with a cross section 60 x 60 mm (2,358 x 2,358 inches). The steel tubing is perforated to attach the lateral surfaces or to add on another shelter. The side surfaces consist of a frame of galvanized steel tubing with a sheet of 4+4 mm (0,15+0,15 inch) laminated safety glass, fixed onto the main frame by galvanized screws.

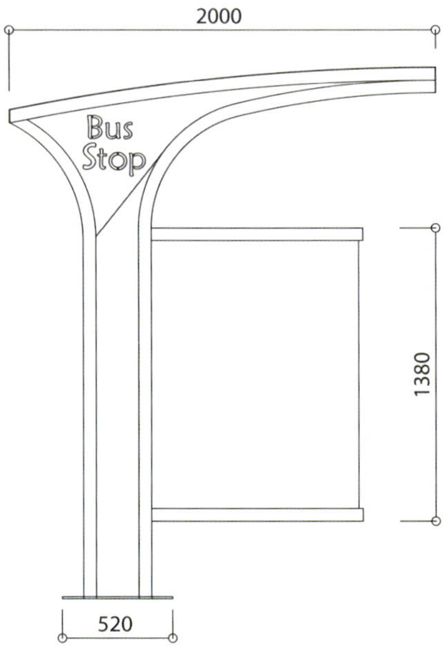

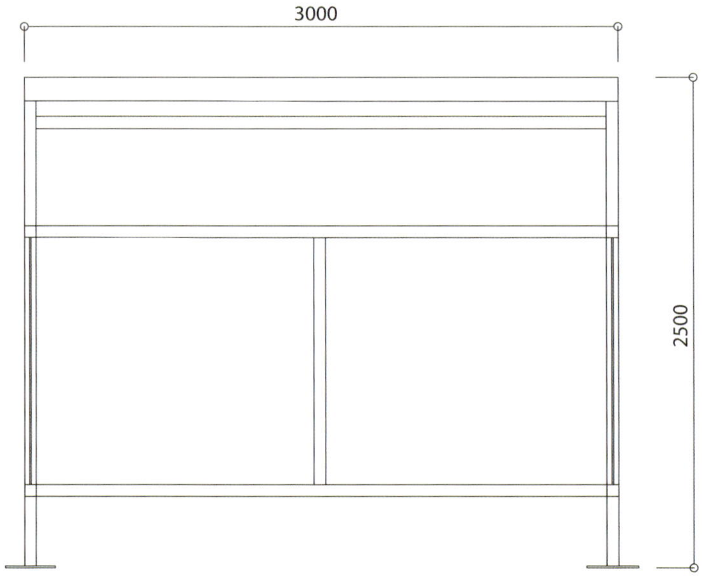

Terminal

Design: David Karásek, Radek Hegmon
Production: mmcité

The roof of this bus stop shelter consists of two wings that hover above cylindrical supporting poles, which they are joined to by a light structural framework. It can be supplied in a choice of different materials, and the special combination of tempered safety glass and galvanized sheet metal profiles suspended under the supporting frame produces a striking effect.

Terminal consists of a galvanized steel structure that comes painted in a range of standard shades. The roofing combines safety glass and profiled (trapezoidal) metal sheeting with an Aluzinc surface. Rainwater collects in the gutter situated under the central beam and drains through the pillars. The facility can be completed with an integrated lighting system, benches, litter bins and timetable holders. It is possible to extend the shelter by the addition of individual modules.

Tramvia

Design: Rafael Cáceres Zurita / Antoni Roselló Til

The idea behind these shelters is to offer a neutral design to counteract the surrounding urban complexity, with simple forms and clean lines, and materials which fit in with the city's collection of street furniture. In addition the aim was to produce a design that could be modular and serialized, so as to construct single or double platforms, different level safety barriers, and so on. The ticket machines, information panels and equipment are all featured in one compact unit so as to avoid the different elements being stretched out all along the platform. The structural approach is fundamental in achieving the essentially light appearance of the shelter: the supports and side enclosures of the equipment unit are set up in the hidden supports of the shelter; the barrier is the most minimal expression of a pedestrian safety barrier; the wind protection is made of glass. The supports which stand at 8 meters above the platform level also feature lighting for the platform and the public way and are an essential part of the structural concept of the shelter. They also act as support elements for the tram's overhead power cables.

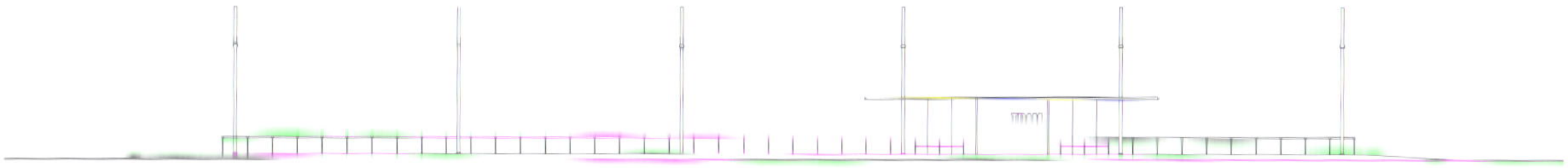

ALZADO ANDÉN LATERAL

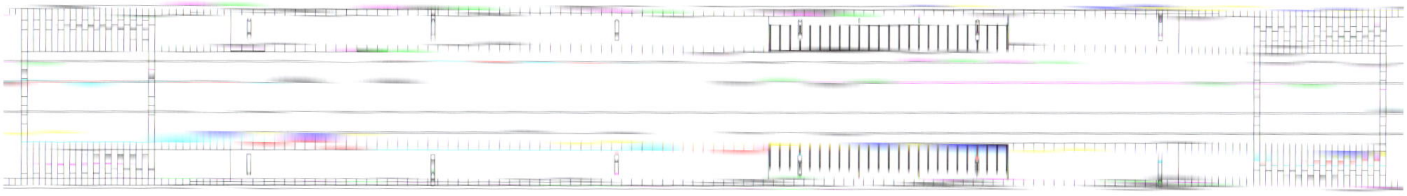

PLANTA ANDÉN LATERAL

Company index

Bd

Bd Ediciones de Diseño S.A.
Pujades 63
08005 Barcelona
Spain

www.bdbarcelona.com
tel: +34 934586909
fax: +34 932073697
email: comercial@bdbarcelona.com
export@bdbarcelona.com

Pages:
36, 53, 78, 94

Botton & Gardiner

Botton and Gardiner urban furniture
37/34-36 Ralph St
Alexandria NSW 2015
Australia

www.bottonandgardiner.com.au
tel: +61 296678100
fax: +61 296672269
email: info@bottonandgardiner.com.au

Pages:
67

DAE

Diseño Ahorro Energético, S.A
Marcel·lí Gené, 16
Pol. Ind. Sant Jordi
08800 Vilanova i la Geltrú
Barcelona
Spain

www.dae.es
tel: +34 938149400
fax: +34 938933358
email: comercial@dae.es
onewton@dae.es

Pages:
15, 88, 91, 125, 132

Escofet

ESCOFET 1886 SA
Ronda Universitat
08007 Barcelona
Spain

www.escofet.com
tel: +34 933185050
fax: +34 934124465
email: informacion@escofet.com

Pages:
24-25, 42, 46, 56, 65, 68-69, 104, 105, 127, 130, 137, 142, 164, 165

Esteva

Esteva
c/Cinemática 9 (Pol. Ind. Los Herreros)
08755 Castellbisbal (Barcelona)
Spain

www.esteva.com
tel: + 34 937720198
fax: +34 937721049

Pages:
157

Estudio Cabeza

Estudio Cabeza
Serrano 1249
C141DEY Buenos Aires
Argentina

www.estudiocabeza.com
tel: +54 1147726183
fax: +54 1147770811
email: info@estudiocabeza.com

Pages:
14, 22-23, 38, 47, 57, 62-63, 82, 86, 136, 170

Euroform

Euroform K. Winkler GmbH
Freiraumausstattung
Eichenstrasse 8a
83083 Riedering
Germany

www.euroform.de
tel: 080364022
fax: 080364024
email: info@euroform.de

Pages:
28

Extremis

Extremis
Weegschede 39 B
8691 Gijverinkhove
Belgium

www.extremis.be
tel: +32 058299725

Pages:
66

Fundició Dúctil Benito

Fundició Dúctil Benito
Via Ausetania, 11
08560 Manlleu (Barcelona)
España

www.fdb.es
tel: +34 938521000
fax: 34 938521001
email: info@fdb.es

Pages:
49, 81, 143

Geohide

GEOHIDE
rue Saint-Martin 7
CH - 1003 Lausanne
Switzerland

www.geohide.ch
www.geohide.eu
tel: +41 213515061
fax: +41 213515025
email: info@geohide.ch
info@geohide.eu

Pages:
61, 73, 89, 97, 117, 120, 155

GHform

GHform
Lundemarksvej 22
DK-4300 Holbæk
Denmark

www.ghform.dk
tel: +45 59440990
fax: +45 59440440
email: mail@ghform.dk

Pages:
18, 33

Ghisamestieri

Ghisamestieri s.r.l.
Via Grande 226
47032 Bertinoro [FC]
Italy

www.ghisamestieri.com
tel: +39 0543462611
fax: +39 0543449111

Pages:
100, 106, 107, 112-113, 118

Hess Form + Licht

Hess Form + Licht
Schlachthausstraße 19 - 19 / 3
D - 78050 Villingen-Schwenningen
Germany

www.hess-form-licht.de
tel: +49 7721920-0
fax: +49 7721 / 920-250
email: hess@hess-form-licht.de

Pages:
102-103

JC Decaux

JCDecaux, London - Paddington Office
Summit House
27 Sale Place
London
W2 1YR
UK

www.jcdecaux.co.uk
tel: 020 7298 8000
email:
angela.mcaveety@jcdecaux.co.uk

Pages:
55, 101, 168

Landscape Forms

Landscape Forms, Inc.
431 Lawndale Ave.
Kalamazoo, MI 49048
USA

www.landscapeforms.com
tel: 8004306209
fax: 2693813455
email: specify@landscapeforms.com

Pages:
19

Larus

Larus
Apartado 100
3 854-909 Albergaria-a-Velha
Portugal

www.larus.pt
tel: 234520600
fax: 234520609
email: larus@mail.telpac.pt

Pages:
147

Louis Poulsen

Louis Poulsen Lighting A/S
International
Sluseholmen 10
DK-2450 Copenhagen
Denmark

www.louis-poulsen.com
tel: +45 70331414
fax: +45 33298646
email: lpl_international@lpmail.com

Pages:
109, 131

Macaedis

Macaedis
ctap, Carretera Olula-Macael, km.1,7
04867 Macael (Almería)
Spain

www.macaedis.com
tel: +34 950126370
fax: +34 950126078
email: info@macaedis.com

Pages:
116, 119, 128, 138, 141

mago: urban

mago: urban
Polígono Industrial Masia d'en Barreres, s/n
08800 Vilanova i la Geltrú
Barcelona
Spain

www.magogroup.com
tel: +34 938148661
fax: +34 938933250
email: info@magogroup.com

Pages:
12-13, 27, 45, 54, 149

Microarquitectura

Microarquitectura
Novel 64
08014
Barcelona
Spain

www.microarquitectura.com
tel: +34 934111191
fax: +34 934912097
email:
comercial@microarquitectura.com

Pages:
115, 150-151

mmcité

mmcité a.s.
Tøída T. Bati 4342
760 01 Zlín
Czech Republic

www.mmcite.cz
tel: +420 577 001 396
tel: +420 577 216 645
fax: +420 577 001 395
email: obchod@mmcite.cz

Pages:
30-31, 43, 58-59, 72, 74, 76, 80, 124, 129, 133, 171, 173

Modo

modo s.r.l
Via Villafranca, 34
35010 - Campodoro - Padova
Italy

www.modoarredo.com
tel: +39 049 9065385
fax: +39 049 9065911

Pages:
20, 154, 156, 159

ORA Centurelli

ORA Centurelli s.r.l.
via C.A. Moriconi, 2
Z.I. Roncaglia
60035 Jesi (AN)
Italy

www.ora.it
tel: 0731 616010
fax: 0731 616010
email: info@ora.it

Pages:
26, 39, 75, 79, 169, 172

Philips

Philips Lighting UK
Philips Centre Guildford Business Park
Guildford
Surrey, GU2 8XH
UK

www.lighting.philips.com
tel: +44 1293 776774
fax: +44 1483 575534

Pages:
99, 110

Richter Spielgeräte

Richter Spielgeräte GmbH
Postfach 54
Simsseestraße 29
83112 Frasdorf
Germany

www.spielgeraete-richter.de
tel: +49 (0) 80 52/17 98-0
fax: +49 (0) 80 52/41 80
email: info@richter-spielgeraete.de

Pages:
158

Runge

Runge GmbH & Co KG
D-49084 Osnabrueck
Germany

www.runge-bank.de
tel: 05 41505520
fax: 05 415055222
email: info@mail-runge.de

Pages:
29, 37, 77

Santa & Cole

Santa & Cole
Parc de Belloch
Ctra. C-251, Km. 5,6
E-08430 La Roca
Spain

www.santacole.com
tel: +34 938462437
fax: +34 938711767
email: info@santacole.com

Pages:
35, 52, 60, 64, 87, 95, 114, 121, 140, 146, 148, 162-163

Siarq

Siarq
Montcada, 31-33, 3,2A
08003
Barcelona
Spain

www.siarq.net
tel: +34 935533913
fax: +34 935533913
email: info@siarq.net

Pages:
96, 108

Street and Park Furniture

www.streetandpark.com.au

Pages:
32, 41, 98

Tecam BCN

TECAM BCN. Mobiliario y Jardineria, SL
Collita, parcela 11, illa 3 - polígono
"Molí de la Bastida"
08191 Rubí
Barcelona
Spain

www.tecambcn.com
tel: +34 936977900
fax: +34 936977901
email: info@tecambcn.com

Pages:
16-17, 34, 48, 83

Tecnología y Diseño Cabanes

Technología & Diseño Cabanes
Pol. Ind. Avanzado
Avda. de la Ciencia 7
13005 Ciudad Real
Spain

www.tdcabanes.es
tel: +34 926251354
fax: +34 926221654
email: info@tdcabanes.com

Pages:
21, 111, 126

Vange

Vange S.A
rue Paradis 62
B-4000 Liege
Belgium

www.vange.be
tel: +32(0)42545570
fax: +32(0)42522037
email: info@vange.be

Pages:
44